T0030469

THE PRISON LADY

THE PRISON LADY

True Stories and Life Lessons
from Both Sides of the Bars

PHYLLIS TAYLOR

sh.
SUTHERLAND
HOUSE
TORONTO, 2022

Sutherland House
416 Moore Ave., Suite 205
Toronto, ON M4G 1C9

Copyright © 2022 by Phyllis Taylor

All rights reserved, including the right to reproduce this book or
portions thereof in any form whatsoever. For information on rights and
permissions or to request a special discount for bulk purchases, please
contact Sutherland House at info@sutherlandhousebooks.com

Sutherland House and logo are registered
trademarks of The Sutherland House Inc.

First edition, October 2022

If you are interested in inviting one of our authors to a live event or
media appearance, please contact sranasinghe@sutherlandhousebooks.com
and visit our website at sutherlandhousebooks.com for more
information about our authors and their schedules.

We acknowledge the support of the Government of Canada.

Manufactured in China
Cover designed by Jordan Lunn and Lena Yang
Book composed by Karl Hunt

Library and Archives Canada Cataloguing in Publication
Title: The prison lady : true stories and life lessons from
both sides of the bars / Phyllis Taylor.
Names: Taylor, Phyllis (Motivational speaker), author.
Identifiers: Canadiana 20220251193 | ISBN 9781989555972 (softcover)
Subjects: LCSH: Taylor, Phyllis (Motivational speaker) |
LCSH: Volunteer workers in corrections—
Ontario—Biography. | LCSH: Motivational speakers—
Ontario—Biography. | LCGFT: Autobiographies.
Classification: LCC HV9308.O5 T39 2022 |
DDC 365/.92—dc23

ISBN 978-1-989555-97-2

Table of Contents

TABLE OF CONTENTS

Dedication

For Emma and Leah: The love of family and friends makes my existence an overwhelming delight, and you are the essence of what it means to love.

Preface

YEARS CAME AND WENT. But they never had decisive markers. Like many of you, I rode the merry-go-round while the years melted together, undefined, and undocumented.

Some would say, "Write a book."

I would say, "I choose not."

Until 2020. In March 2020, the entire universe became a screwy sci-fi flick. In domino fashion, countries around the world were advised to shelter in place. Illness. Death. Loss. Life sucked and hearts ached.

COVID-19 forced us to think and reflect, so I put down my makeup and picked up my pen. In this book, I bring you the best of me at the worst of times, with the bold authentic flavour I value in others.

This book is a blend of the highlights and lowlights that have threaded my life and a decade of prisoners who have touched my heart. My personal and intimate stories intersect with inspirations that promote healing, provide hope and suggest intentional change.

Inspiration is circular. In responding to prisoners, I found answers. We must dare to reach outward and listen inward.

These chapters provide flexible guidance, strategies, and tested formulas that will provide the growth you desire and the change you seek. Read the book and do the work. Partner with me. Your upgrade will be noticed and admired.

The lessons in this book are meant to awaken the soul and gently poke you into forward-thinking. My game plan: to enlighten, entertain and provide a better understanding of prison life and of prisoners. Prisoners are mostly just people looking to tidy up an unspeakable life or a rude beginning.

My personal story begins with its own struggle. I was a young girl who suffered father abuse in a world that had no idea it was happening or didn't care. This is a story of courage and empathy that emerged from a risky and troubled childhood. My childhood inspired a desperate need to connect with others—especially the disenfranchised—and to help them.

When I became a motivational speaker, my aspiration was to touch hearts and grow minds. Remarkably, as I spoke, they listened. In prison, I saw badass narcissism morph into care and kindness.

My role now is to educate the weary, read to the illiterate and stop the bleeding. This work exposes the raw emotions of those who suffer. Emotions that rewire my soul as I hear about their high crimes in low places. Their gratitude encourages me to work harder and to do more. There is a mystical, unpolished gift in these budding friendships.

But what about success, you may ask?

These are my success markers. He unburdens a dark moment. She has an awakening. He shows concern for my welfare. My God, those moments are exhilarating.

Woven into this book is an invitation to gain cognitive insight. An opportunity for enlightenment and change. If you are looking to be entertained and moved in the same moment, read on, my friends. And enjoy!

CHAPTER ONE

There goes another life

"DAMN! WHO'S CALLING on Saturday night?" I sighed, throwing my fork down in protest.

A fluffy knish and A warm side of gravy await me. Saturday is sacred: Pancer's Deli and movie mania. Wentworth, the badass prison series, is all fired up waiting for me to push play. A knish and a movie; the perfect duo for a carb-craving drama queen.

After a protracted fight with my calorie restrictions, the anticipation of dinner was a brain pleaser. But as I leaned back, put my feet up and was about to exhale, the phone rang.

Despite shrieking "screw off," the damn thing persisted. By now, my fiancé John understood that 'screw off' was not an intentional mating call. I mean, really, kiss 'n knish?

Grabbing the phone, I saw: 'Unknown Caller.' Don't answer, I thought. But curiosity killed the knish.

"Hello, Phyllis, how are you this evening?" Unknown Caller asked with a shaky voice.

"I'm fine. Who is this, may I ask?" Always a sucker for a deep voice.

"It's Jason, Jason Marshall. You know me. From prison."

"Of course, Jason. How did you get my number?"

1

"You gave it to me."

The prisons instruct us never to provide inmates with personal data, but life has made me quite comfortable with breaking the rules. Always for a good cause, though. And Jason is a damn good cause.

"Jason, how are you? It's been ages."

"Yes. Two years," he said, pausing, and then added, "I'm not doing well, Phyllis. It's not that I'm going to off myself or anything, but I'm in rough shape. Really bad."

When someone tells you they're not thinking about suicide, that's exactly what they're thinking. Words provide hints, but the voice reveals emotion. Feelings of desperation in this case.

No knish for you, I thought. "

What's going on, Jason?"

"Things aren't going well, Phyllis."

"Tell me more."

"I messed up. Suffered a brain injury playing football. My parents are . . . can't even see my daughter these days."

"Jason, have you been drinking?"

"Um, nah."

"Jason?"

"Well, yeah. I've fallen down. I didn't even know who to call . . . or where to turn tonight."

Shortly before Jason and I met, he had suffered a psychotic break that mixed poorly with alcohol. Jason had come after Mom and Dad with a bad attitude and a sharp knife. And so, at thirty and a bit, Jason, a chartered accountant, was convicted of assault causing bodily harm and sentenced to Maplehurst Correctional Centre for a few years. Jason's mom had minor battle scars. Jason earned a criminal record.

There goes another life.

Jason was like dessert at Maplehurst. Young, intelligent and pretty are not prison assets. These qualities cause acute jealousy and are a magnet for horny bastards. Although inmates don't typically like pretty boys, they have no problem raping them. Jason was targeted for misery and sustained a brutal sexual violation.

Ferociously molested by an angry cellmate one night, Jason was left bleeding until a guard found him during a routine headcount. As one would expect, this horrific ordeal left deep emotional scars. The prison had failed Jason and he needed a friend.

We met soon after when Jason was transferred from Maplehurst to the Ontario Correctional Institute (OCI). He is my son's age and, over time, a friendship grew between us. With his good looks, charming personality and an open willingness to share, Jason was easy to like.

So, he became a project of mine, and when he left OCI a few years later, Jason was on a healing journey. He had a promising future that was significantly better than most prisoners. But tonight, Jason was sinking into despair. And everything he had accomplished had somehow gone to shit.

Talking to Jason made me feel sad. With my mind stretching to think outside the cell, I desperately wanted to help, but the COVID-19 pandemic had us all sheltering in place. The only ammunition I had was a charging cell phone and some finely honed conversation skills. So, I just kept talking.

"Jason, are you alone?" I asked, praying he wasn't.

"I live with my parents." (The same parents Jason once attacked.)

An hour passed. And then two. I was terrified to hang up, fearing that hopelessness would win. My empathy engine was in overdrive.

Unlike most people in the prison system, Jason was born into wealth and power. His father, William, a retired English professor and philanthropist, was busy donating new wings to old hospitals. As a pastime, William managed both his money and the neighbourhood hospitals.

Jason had suffered from mild father abuse as a child. I find it notable that even our most sophisticated elitists can screw up their kids. Certainly, my dad did it on a lot less money.

"Jason, we can't talk when you're drunk."

"Okay," he whispered.

"So, here's what we'll do. Do you trust me?"

"Yes, yes I do," came the resounding response.

"Jason, I need you to promise me that you'll go to sleep when we hang up." I was begging for sober time so we could have a more productive conversation later. "And then call me in the morning. I will be here."

"I can do that," he whispered as the drink melted away.

"And one more thing, Jason. Please put your dad on the phone."

"Okay, hold on please." He was shockingly compliant and desperate for guidance. Good.

A moment later, I was having a friendly chat with Jason's dad. Damn, it's hard not to judge. But despite William's serious demeanour and ego-speak, we got along fine. In that moment, I had no pride. Come to think of it, pride really isn't my thing. And so, William and I chatted as if we were old buddies.

About an hour into our conversation and timid about what William might say, I marshalled the courage to plead help for Jason. Although I received no real commitment from William, I had made him aware that his son could be suicidal.

Ending the conversation, William formally thanked me for my interest in his son and my service in the prison system. That was indeed lovely, but I wasn't convinced that my late-night presentation would stick or that it was a yes to helping his boy.

According to plan, Jason called me the next morning. He was shaky but sober. "My dad said he'd pay for Homewood. It's a go."

I heard fear in every syllable.

Homewood Health Centre is a treatment and rehabilitation centre for the very rich. They describe themselves as the Canadian leader in mental health and addiction services and say that they are redefining mental health and addiction services to help Canadians live healthier, more productive and more fulfilling lives.

"But only if I can convince him I'm dead serious," he added.

Interesting choice of words, I thought.

"I desperately need this chance, Phyllis."

Jason was emotional and compelling. Perhaps he had hit rock bottom.

Many believe that those suffering with a drugs or alcohol must get worse before getting better. Unfortunately, things get a lot worse when someone hits bottom. Bottom looks different for everyone and some just keep on digging.

Addicts in recovery say there's a significant moment when they awaken: the light that results in achieving sobriety. For someone who doesn't understand addiction, in this case Jason's dad, it was difficult for him to understand and even more difficult to determine whether Jason was serious about recovery.

"Awesome, Jason. Amazing! Are you serious about getting clean? More importantly, are you serious about staying clean? We have been down this road before, my friend."

"I hope so," was the best I could get from a frightened and uncertain young man. One who may already have given up.

"Listen carefully, Jason. Here's the thing. You have a daughter, right? What's her name?"

"Victoria." I heard the name and a smile.

"She's five."

She was the same age as Emma, my eldest granddaughter.

"Jason, you have two options. Two critically different options. Please listen very carefully. You can either destroy Victoria's life by maintaining the victim stance and continuing your alcohol fest, or you can get help, get clean and be her hero. Victoria's hero!"

"I never thought of it quite like that," he said, slowly enunciating every word.

"Your daughter needs a father, Jason. Make her proud of you and be a part of her life. Be the hero of your life too, Jason. You can do this. I know you can. I believe in you. You are not alone."

It seemed that a powerless mind was registering a glimmer of hope. My morning enthusiasm and passion fully kicked in as I continued to plead with Jason.

Within days, Jason was admitted to Homewood as an emergency resident. For weeks, I sent Jason encouraging text messages, but got no reply. I emailed William and received no response. As my concern for Jason mounted, my confidence was fading.

Finally, two months later, I received a text message from Jason: "Still in Homewood and doing well. Treatment is immersion. Will graduate Homewood February 23. Am going to be Victoria's hero."

It's fascinating how earning someone's trust and providing encouragement can change the trajectory of their life. There is nothing more exhilarating. If you have the opportunity to throw a light on someone's darkness, there's no need to think it over.

That's how we roll.

CHAPTER TWO

When one door closes . . .

S OMETIMES GETTING FIRED CAN be the best worst thing that ever happens. My work with prisoners is a calling—a perfect fit with my personality and lived experience (more about that later). But I spent decades doing something else. Working myself up from receptionist to junior legal secretary, and from senior secretary to paralegal until, at the peak of my law firm career, I became a technical writer and training specialist.

The job was to teach legal and non-legal software programs to the men and women of "McBillion LLP." Whatever it took to run their practice, I was their gal. And this distinctive teaching position came with a writing opportunity to personally author each of the corresponding user guides. Along with all of this, I was provided with a glorious training centre.

The position included an extensive educational benefit package. Boom! I began to upgrade my education, taking both college and university courses. Being highly driven and craving education, I attended what was then called Ryerson University to study journalism, George Brown College to study teaching, training and counselling and the University of Toronto to study philosophy, thereby advancing my critical-thinking bits.

This extraordinary career stoked my brain and energized my heart. The position encouraged creativity, utilized my writing skills and commanded an audience. I lived to teach and I loved to teach. The job defined and completed me. My upgrade plan also gave me a chance for a new hobby. After years of teaching Toronto's finest, I began competitive public speaking, which won me numerous local and national awards.

During this time, my personal life was also under construction. I met my second husband, Philip, after a decade of dating and soul-crushing relationships. By then, my focus was on finding a lovely guy, but I failed to find a compatible one. A compatible guy would have been intelligent and emotionally sound. Instead, I settled down with Philip, a forty-ish mild-mannered Italian man.

Philip was supposed to be an Italian Stallion. A joke, right? Only the joke was on me. Philip's first marriage had broken his devoted, family-man heart. His wife had indulged in a vigorous affair, which seriously damaged Philip. And this damage manifested itself in the most sacred place—the bedroom. But I had heard that Italians were stallions. And Philip had heard that once you marry a Jewish girl, you can forget about sex. Turns out we both had the wrong idea.

After twenty years married to Philip and an enjoyable thirty years spent working for McBillions, my career came to an agonizing, abrupt end. My days of reporting to Lorie Blundon, a woman who I had come to love (despite our respectful head butting), ended when the firm decided to fire Lorie and hire Katherine. Katherine would become my new director— but not for long.

Katherine was overwhelmed and inexperienced.

Before long, I began to intimidate Katherine as she became aware that I was highly respected and clearly knowledgeable. I had mastered the training world and Katherine was nervous. Not because I was smart or special, but because I cherished my job and was a devout software enabler.

So, before leaving on vacation, I felt that it was my ethical and professional duty to inform Natalie, our human resources director, that the firm had made a bad hiring decision. I respectfully submitted that Katherine must go. I was proud of my quick discovery and confident that Natalie would follow my advice. After all, I had provided several concrete examples of Katherine's stupidity. But I was wrong. It turned out that Natalie had personally interviewed and hired Katherine herself. Clearly, I had fucked up.

Unaware, I went on a glorious Caribbean cruise, and upon returning to the office three weeks later, I was let go. There is never an elegant way to fire someone, but I will never forget what Natalie said as she gingerly handed me my walking papers and noticed the colour drain from my face.

"What I'm about to do is very bad for the firm, but very good for you."

That moment when shock morphs into awareness was like something out of a made for TV movie. This horrific marker came after thirty years with the firm, decades of building a department and an enormous amount of pride. All of it was packed into a single cardboard box, and I was escorted out of the building in a painful and humiliating walk of shame.

It was crushing.

Shocked by this epic fail, I was devastated and embarrassed. With tears streaming down my cheeks, a numbness I had only heard about and in deep emotional pain, I made my way to the neighbouring law firm where my daughter, Mel, worked.

After mumbling a brief explanation, I presented Melanie with the manila envelope that housed their reasons for judgment and terms of settlement. After a laboured reading of my termination agreement, Mel bounded from her seat, clapped her hands in the air, and squealed with delight.

"Mom, you just won the freaking lottery!" An interesting perspective.

Fortunately, the firm was generous. A severance package, used to pacify the guilty conscience of a firing squad, came with clauses to neither compete nor disclose and a healthy money deal that would soon enable me to fulfill a lifelong dream.

Later than afternoon, still heartsick, I taxied over to Lynda's. My high school friend, now a housewife, welcomed the news I'd been fired. Since I was "paid out big time," we could do retirement together by simply shopping at Costco and lunching with ladies. I cannot overstate how unappealing that sounded. It seemed as if everyone was happy but me.

I remember making my bed the next morning and thinking: What the hell am I to do with the rest of my life? And then I thought: Use your skills. Volunteer. But I had absolutely no idea where to begin.

Minutes later, the phone rang. "Hey, it's Lyndyloo. Oprah's coming to Toronto. $250 a pop. We're going!"

"Not me," I protested, "No money, no interest."

"No money?" she bellowed in her don't-be-nuts tone. "You got a huge payout."

Begrudgingly, I agreed to escort Lynda to the Oprah fest. Thank goodness.

CHAPTER THREE

Oprah is coming to town

W HEN THE DAY ARRIVED, we dragged ourselves down to the Air Canada Centre to stand in the rain for six hours with several thousand exceedingly friendly, Oprah-inspired folk. I was overwhelmed with boredom until security announced, "We're going in folks."

Seating was not reserved, so a kind of demented stampede ensued. Fiercely elbowing our way into the arena, we landed two tight seats, hundreds of rows from the stage. We could barely see Oprah. But we were there, and Lynda was happy.

The Oprah "Lifeclass" focused on gratitude. The speaker lineup consisted of Tony Robbins, Deepak Chopra, Iyanla Vanzant and Bishop T. D. Jakes. Moderating and interviewing this group of luminaries was our beloved Oprah Winfrey. Everyone was passionate about the event. Except me.

We were comfortably seated when Oprah began the guest speaker introductions. But I was much more interested in her additional guests: six ladies who were doing time at the Indiana Women's Prison and were shown onstage via Skype.

These inspiring women, known as The Six Pack, touched my heart in a way that I can only describe as an awakening. They were entirely captivated by the notable speakers, and I was captivated by them. These gals were close to the door, which meant that they would soon be finished their prison sentences and faced with new and greater challenges. After serving many years inside, navigating freedom takes formidable effort.

For The Six Pack, or anyone leaving prison, life is extraordinarily difficult. Parole carries heavy restrictions and securing employment with a prison record is immensely challenging. Many prisoners report that they are frightened when leaving prison. Often inmates are released into a different world than the one they left.

For inmates serving longer sentences, it's common to arrive home only to find that family and friends have either moved on or passed away. A limited support system creates even greater challenges when transitioning back into society, especially if one only knows the mindset that put them behind bars. Some still suffer from the guilt and shame of their crimes and often experience a homecoming of hopelessness.

The obstacles that parolees face are weightier than the strengths they acquire in prison. Those arrested as minors, and who have served lengthy sentences, leave prison with limited life experience. When they are released, the simple tasks that we take for granted are often unattainable. The result is constant fear and anxiety.

Tony Robbins was the first to speak, but I confess that my attention was fixated on The Six Pack. With each speaker, I studied the women's facial expressions, body language and level of enthusiasm. From time to time, a speaker would respectfully interact with the ladies. They were fully engaged, transparently sharing their own personal stories and eager to heal. There was no doubt that they were hopeful, planning for a better tomorrow and grateful to be a part of Oprah's Lifeclass.

And by now so was I.

Spellbound by the women's storytelling, my heart felt heavy and light at the same time. I had never been so altogether moved. It was both a gift and a blessing. It was divine and it was by design. I wanted to speak with them, reach out to them, hug them but, most of all, I wanted to help them.

Bishop TD Jakes was the final speaker. Once he took the stage, I began to relax into his presentation and absorb his lesson on gratitude. As philosophy and mind-body healing came together in his remarks, my mood was euphoric. It felt as if Bishop Jakes was speaking directly to me. Neurons were firing in my brain as I sat there in awe of his teaching.

The Bishop ended with: "Others can inspire you, but ultimately the only thing that empowers you is what lies within you and learning how to better utilize what you've been given."

I monitored The Six Pack intently for their reaction. Several of the women lit up with what seemed to be some sort of light. I understood that along with six inspiring women, my restorative soul had taking root. It was clear that this moment was pivotal and that it was permanently altering my psyche. A desperate but somehow hopeful group of women from a prison in Indiana had opened my heart and redirected my future. Forever.

Suddenly, involuntarily, I slapped my knee and sprung from my seat. It was a eureka moment.

"Holy fuck, that's what I'll do!"

Hurray for Lynda, hurray for Oprah, hurray for Bishop TD Jakes and The Six Pack! Phyllis is coming to prison town.

CHAPTER FOUR

Calling all prisons

RETURNING HOME FROM THE Oprah event, I was electrified. (Lynda was mystified.) I was riveted, thinking about my career as a motivational speaker in the prison system. Thoughts were racing through my mind and excitement was mounting.

It never occurred to me that I might not have the skills required for the role or that I couldn't sell my mission statement. With confidence and the determination to succeed, I believed that my project would gather momentum or at least be given an entry level pass.

I was sure that, having been fired from my teaching position, a prison career was the universe balancing out. Or that a higher power was at the wheel. After all, my severance payout was cushion enough to pursue this dream.

Confidence is a game changer. It's an inner awareness that comes when you face challenges and experience success. As a learned behaviour, confidence will generate a lovely existence, especially when you add enough energy and oxygen to encourage positive thinking.

My strategy was to google all prisons within a fifty-kilometre radius and volunteer my services as a motivational speaker. I wanted to speak directly with the inmates, but I had no idea what I might speak about. That should be fine.

Invigorated, I searched "prisons near me" and called each one. I asked to speak with a volunteer services person, but failed to reach anyone. So, I left voice messages. Actually, I left a message trail clear across the city limits and into neighbouring towns.

A few days later, I received a call from Lori Shank, the Volunteer Services and Educational Director at a local prison. "What is it you'd like to do?" Lori inquired.

"I'm a motivational speaker," I said, trying to sound confident and humble at once.

"Well, we don't have anything like that here."

"What do you have, Lori?"

"Yoga and AA."

"Perfect, my body of work will go beautifully with yoga," I said. Thinking: what body of work are you talking about?

"I don't really think we have an opportunity for you here, but perhaps you might just drop by for a chat," Lori said dismissively. "How about Friday at noon, would that work?"

"Perfect," I said, trying to sound calm. "Thank you, Lori."

She asked me to send along my resume and hung up.

Moments later, I was on Facebook announcing that I'd been granted an interview at a local prison. I asked my friends for serious prayers, settled for some emoji prayer icons and told my followers to stay tuned for further developments. Exactly how CNN would announce Breaking News.

And, like the gods of volunteerism were channeling me that day, I received a private message from Lorie Blundon, my former director. We had kept in touch after she left the firm and had formed a meaningful personal relationship. Lorie was now working in Human Resources at Durham College and asked if my prison interview was at the Metro East Detention Centre. (It was.) Lorie explained that she had a contact at Metro East—a man who had recently graduated Durham College and been placed at Metro as a Correctional Officer.

This coincidence is a chance to reflect on the idea of a divine plan; an idea I wholeheartedly believe. In my Jewish culture we use the word bashert, which translates from Yiddish as destiny or fate. We often invoke this concept when speaking of romantic fate but I was planning a prison gig and everything was falling into place.

I arrived for the interview wearing my finest volunteer ensemble. Okay, maybe I was a tad overdressed. It's an intimidating building but, clearly, I was the happiest person ever to enter a prison. You know, that feeling when you walk through a door and it just feels right.

As I entered Metro East, I faced two Control Desk Officers. No one smiled but me. After a brief identification ceremony, someone notified Lori Shank of my arrival.

With piercing blue eyes and a pretty face, Lori was a soft-spoken woman who seemed kind. Together we navigated the sally port doors. The controlled entry system, common in high security settings, has a holding space between two sliding walls. Neither wall can be opened at the same time. As both walls shut, attendees are temporarily trapped, pending clearance.

The experience, for me, was heavenly. A door was opening to my new life.

The second sliding wall opened to the administrative offices, and we walked towards Lori's basic, brick-walled office. We chatted easily. Not having been on an interview in decades, I had mentally prepared myself for a challenging, in-depth interrogation. I had rehearsed my body language, tone and many selling points to convince Lori that Metro East needed a Phyllis. But as I sat in her office awaiting this opportunity, Lori smiled at me. With virtually no exchange about my qualifications or goals, she had reached a verdict.

"So," Lori announced, "I've figured out exactly what we'll do with your program."

I gasped. Only on the inside, of course, as I sat motionless and expressionless in front of her. Excitedly, I was thinking: Holy Crap. And then: Oy. I managed a controlled smile without jumping off the walls.

"Would you work on anger management with the prisoners?" Lori asked.

Anger Management, I thought.

The only experience I had with anger was a stage four angry father whom no one could manage. But I told Lori to consider it done, and I would go home to research and write. Thanks to continuing education, I knew how to create a lesson plan and write an instructional manual.

"May I review a draft of your Anger Management booklet in a month's time?" Lori continued.

"Yes, of course," I managed.

"Beautiful," she said. "And we'll see how it goes."

I nodded thinking: time to prove yourself, Phyllis. Let's roll.

Lori explained that the men would each receive a copy of my booklet, but there were to be no pictures, sexy language or staples. I later learned that prisoners use staples to apply their homemade prison tattoos, and I was not to be their staple supplier.

Two months after being fired from a prestigious law firm, my career took a more meaningful tack. Transitioning from a swanky office environment to a musty prison cell was extraordinarily thrilling, surreal and a bit like being in The Twilight Zone. I was exchanging marble floors for concrete walls and forgoing posh bathrooms for gas station style toilets. So much to explore. Nothing would ever be the same again. Happily, I parked my life in front of my laptop to research and write about anger management.

Commitment to a goal means overcoming all obstacles. Even normal everyday living is an obstacle. I was relentlessly researching anger, writing and rewriting my booklet, always striving for excellence. I knew that if I brought it, if I stretched myself beyond my outer limits, this project could truly make a difference.

Weeks later, with Lori now in possession of my draft anger management booklet, I was asked to attend intensive training for new prison employees and volunteers. There were four trainees in our group, who were background checked and vetted like we were going undercover for the FBI. It seemed harder to break into prison than out.

The training was sensational—until it came to the hostage taking lesson. Although we were told that this training was strictly a formality, it was unnerving. The trainers told us that inmates pay close attention to the behaviour of staff and would easily exploit the weaknesses of personnel and the facility if they could. We were told to stay alert for any possible threat or security breach. We were also told to learn the emergency procedures in advance, as there would be no time to refer to the manual in case of a hostage situation. We were told to act quickly and not be afraid to think outside the box in order to keep ourselves safe.

Our training also included a tour of the cell block. Imagine a long hallway. One side is lined with prison cells and the other is a concrete brick wall. In preparation, our instructor warned us not to walk on the cell side of the hallway and stick close to the brick wall. The idea was to stay safe, ensuring that no prisoner would harm us.

That seemed like a good idea.

As we approached the cell block, our instructor announced, "Don't look at the men. This is not a zoo." Predictably, as we approached the cell block, everyone peered at the men as if it were a zoo. They were everywhere. All shapes, all sizes, all colours, and all clad in orange. It was a metaphorical zoo.

And so it began. I was assigned to a nine-by-nine foot room (designed for lawyer-client meetings) that contained one metal table and four metal chairs bolted to the cement floor. I sat down and contemplated the other three chairs.

Just then, four men in handcuffs and shackles were presented to me. On arrival, two delivery guards roughly pushed them up against the wall and proceeded to pat them down. It was creepy, and I was very unnerved. But I was ready. When the prisoners were released to me, I explained that we had three chairs and four men. Therefore, they would need to play musical chairs while I remained seated.

My instructions continued. "Gentlemen, how about every fifteen minutes, one of you stand up and respectfully gesture your chair to the man who's standing. Would that work for you guys?"

They nodded without emotion.

It's interesting that although the lesson was a bit challenging, they handled the musical chair routine with complete grace. The lesson in respect and sharing was marvellous, but the anger management script wasn't getting us very far.

After three weeks of this routine, Lori explained to me that Metro East is not a prison, but a detention centre; a place where prisoners are held awaiting trial. Naturally, inmates in detention are fearful, nervous and uncertain. That certainly explains why my Metro group had little or no attention span.

Lori gently went on to say that my anger lesson really wasn't transferring too well and that I would do better in a 'real prison,' (officially called a correctional institute), better suited to my teaching efforts.

In other words, Lori was saying goodbye.

So, in the spirit of bashert, as the sally port door to Metro East was closing, another opened. Just days after leaving Metro, I received a call from Penny McLean of Vanier, a prison for women.

The Vanier Centre for Women, located in Milton, Ontario houses approximately 125 prisoners, many of whom have unique needs. Often these women suffer from mental health disabilities, addiction and post-traumatic stress disorder, mostly rooted in trauma that was experienced at home or in their communities.

Penny vowed that if I enjoyed the men, I would love the women. She requested that we meet. I suspected that Lori Shank had buzzed Penny to tell her I'd be a great fit. And in that moment, I was absolutely certain that the universe had conspired to further my dream.

Penny and I met the following week, and I agreed to deliver a trial presentation. She said that if my inaugural presentation went well, she might consider a regular gig.

And just like that, orange became the new Phyllis.

CHAPTER FIVE

The women of Vanier

V ANIER IS A maximum-security prison. After entering the place, visitors undergo a full body scan for external and internal contraband. The scanner, a fancy new high-tech miracle, detects swallowed or inserted items. That's right, it shoots clear through the body and peeks right inside your vagina. Sweet!

During training, our instructor advised us to "go dark." That means leaving all personal belongings in the car (no purse, no phone). Upon clearance, our keys and coats are placed in a locker, and the locker key is to be kept well-hidden. Keys are weapons too.

The day had arrived for me to deliver my first presentation to an audience of women. Penny would assemble about 100 prisoners for my induction, and, of course, she would attend too. Perhaps I should be intimidated.

The topic: Positive Thinking.

That Tuesday, I arrived at the prison energized and nervous. This was it. I was living the dream. I would deliver the best presentation ever known to women and then float away on a chariot of hope pulled by white horses.

Except, as I headed towards the prison, I realized that all of my materials and equipment were missing—they were locked in the car.

I felt a nightmare-level panic attack take hold. A feeling of alarm. Dread. Momentary brain fog. And then, uncontrollable shaming self-talk: Oh my God, you're a loser. You can't even remember your materials? Now you blew it.

A pause.

A deep breath and another thought, this one deliberate. C'mon, you're teaching positive thinking! You've got this. Okay. Now take a few deep breaths and imagine an engaged and alert audience . . . and Penny smiling.

Within seconds, I calmed myself enough to realize that my keys were actually in my coat pocket, not locked in the car. I walked back to the vehicle, opened the door and retrieved my precious materials.

An hour later, I delivered the best damn presentation of my life. In a vulnerable wrap-up, I revealed how I had thought I'd foolishly locked my materials in the car, yet managed to turn my silly misstep into a learning opportunity. I told the ladies about my negative self-talk and how I had applied a positive thinking hack to arrive at a winning outcome.

In that moment, they were fully engaged and I could see them thinking. It felt wonderful. As I thanked them for allowing me into their home, the group of 100 orange-suited women stood, smiled and applauded. They were directing gratitude my way with a level of enthusiasm that was deeply humbling.

Public speaking was better with cheerleaders. A unique audience of attentive women desperate for hope. Perhaps the kind of hope that would begin the healing process and encourage change. For all of us.

During discussion period, one woman asked, "Why didn't anyone tell me this stuff when I was growin' up? I sure coulda used someone like you to tell me I had them choices."

Also in the audience was Destiny, affectionately known as "Trucker" referring to her strong preference for turning tricks at truck stops. A thirty-seven-year-old natural beauty, Destiny had blond wavy hair that flowed down her back to slightly above her butt. With a body that wouldn't quit, Destiny was gorgeous.

She had been a part time prostitute, a part time drug dealer and a career-minded criminal. And she would become my friend and teacher. Over time, I learned that Destiny was a talented soul with a flair for poetry that was insightful but heartbreaking. A deeply painful childhood had given her profound insight into the human mind and deviant behaviour. I often wondered what Destiny might have become had she been offered a stable home and a loving parent.

After my inaugural presentation, Penny surrendered. She granted me a permanent Tuesday gig, a room with no view and an assistant to help with setup. I was granted carte blanche to research, write and deliver on any topic that I deemed appropriate and prison-worthy. And each lesson was to be accompanied by a supporting booklet.

This was a tall ask that demanded an enormous time commitment. I was required to produce booklet after booklet of life lessons. It was worth it though, because months later I learned that the women of Vanier treasured these little handouts. And, when a woman went off campus (left prison), she would share her materials with a troubled friend or a little sister.

If you've watched the female prison series, *Orange is the New Black*, you know Vanier. The Netflix series is remarkably realistic with its lesbian loves and miserable bullies. Unlike the character Red in the TV series, our cook was supervised and less likely to poison her least favoured guests.

Vanier boasts an ample population of incompetent and insecure women who suck up to guards. It's always about a self-serving agenda that routinely includes ratting out your bestie. I was treated to a crash course in humanity and life-affirming reasons to teach.

"Tuesdays with Phyllis" began with Destiny as my informal prison consultant. In the early days, I needed her to translate the lingo and explain how these women tick. My learning curve seemed endless, but Destiny never lost patience with me. In fact, she seemed to find me wonderfully refreshing. Destiny and I were friends and her honest feedback gave me a reliable measure of progress.

Destiny constantly assured me that I was making a difference for the women of Vanier. She validated my lessons and guided me on my journey. Her strong endorsement and passionate counsel were humbling and exhilarating.

Studies show that leading a meaningful life is mandatory in the pursuit of happiness. When you shine a light on others, they often shine one back. I have also learned that those who have experienced the most pain are often the best teachers. The person I am today is largely because of the many "Destinys" who put their trust in me with their own special blend of kindness.

As we got better acquainted, Destiny explained that she was born in a biker house. I wasn't quite sure what that meant. Destiny explained that her father was unaccounted for and her biker mama gave birth to her in the Hells Angels clubhouse—and then left. It seemed that her mom needed a fresh start.

The clubhouse was no place for kids. Destiny said she was raised by the bikers who were "doing Mom a favour." Sadly, this favour included abuse on every level, including sexual abuse. Deviants often prey on the most readily available victims. Disgustingly selfish and horribly evil. But Destiny was a survivor. She would have given anything for a brief conversation with her mom. She'd enjoyed a few special visits in past years and learned her mother now lived in Vancouver's East Side and was dealing drugs. Destiny had lost touch with her, but hoped to find her once she left prison.

The day Destiny told me her story, we held hands and cried for a very long time.

One afternoon, Destiny didn't make it to class. I later learned that she was experiencing severe depression and wanted privacy. I was teaching intimacy and relationships that day, a lesson on emotional closeness and connectedness. Suddenly, I spotted two inmates begin to fondle one another in their secret places. That's right, fondle. Front row centre.

That day gave new definition to inappropriate behaviour, but I stayed calm and lived to regret it. With absolutely no idea how to handle this development, I did nothing. But mentally, I was alternating between thoughts to "stay calm" or "scream loud."

After class, I reported the incident to Penny during our what-happened-today debrief. After listening intently, Penny looked at me as if I were missing a brain.

"Do you do that in public?" she asked.

A soft "no" slipped from my lips.

"So why did you allow them to do it?" she asked, respectful but firm.

I explained that I had frozen and, before I could thaw, they had stopped. Penny gently insisted that next Tuesday I discuss classroom boundaries and appropriate group behaviour. When the day arrived, I did just that and, despite the ladies' quiet demeanour, a few sideways smiles made it the most awkward prison moment on record—my record.

At Vanier, I earned a reputation for being the motivational speaker who cared. Sitting at the computer for hours each day cranking out booklet after booklet was gruelling, but I knew that this work was meaningful and outrageously rewarding. I find it intriguing that as a motivational speaker, there is seldom a session where I don't learn as valuable a lesson as I teach.

While studying human behaviour, healing and growth for the prisoners, I began to notice my own personal growth. It was slow at first, but here's my dirty little secret. Teaching lawyers had been a wonderful career. The job defined me and elevated my confidence. But looking back, I realize that I was an intellectual snob; I was demanding and somewhat impatient. Still, with all those filthy little flaws, I had a remarkably good, work-in-progress heart. While those close to me acknowledged this warm heart, none could quite figure out the peculiar blend of a soft heart and a sharp tongue.

Experiencing life with more humanity, I found myself loving more deeply, listening more intently, striving to exude kindness and enjoying more meaningful relationships. I began to see that in researching benevolence and teaching compassion, I, too, was healing. By coaching the children of a deviant god, I was developing my own emotional quotient. I am still a developing story of ample weaknesses, someone who makes mistakes and screws up nicely. But every life is precious and deserves a second chance.

Week after week, my relationship with the audience deepened. Together we learned and laughed. We embraced a healing trajectory that we were destined to journey. Working with prisoners was a humbling way of developing and deepening my own character, something that was long overdue. Slowly, my lifelong wounds began to heal. And my ability to help others was forever enhanced.

There were precious moments that I'll cherish forever. And I was humbled when, after two years at Vanier, I was awarded 'Volunteer of the Year.' My daughter Melanie escorted me to the award dinner, which made it the proudest professional day of my life. It felt surreal to have her attend prison with me but it gave Melanie the opportunity to speak with several of the inmates, who expressed gratitude for my visits. The feeling of reward that evening warmed my soul.

As many know, there's a prison inside the prison. You may have heard it referred to as "the hole," "segregation" or "solitary confinement." These references all refer to a lonely place inside the prison walls—protective custody.

A few years after I began working with Vanier's general population, I was offered an opportunity to work with the women in protective custody. These women are kept apart because they are high profile and could fall victim to other prisoners or, conversely, they are a danger to themselves or others. Most of these women have received their final sentence, but some are merely in custody pending trial. Many of them suffer from severe intellectual and emotional inadequacies and most have suffered a life of abuse.

This was a huge vote of confidence in me from Penny McLean at Vanier.

I was assigned to teach these women on Tuesday evenings and a new program initiative began. I spent Tuesday afternoons with the women in "gen pop," enjoyed an ice cream dinner at McDonald's, and headed back to prison in the evening to teach the women in protective custody. Clearly, Tuesday was my favourite day of the week.

My heart ached for these victims and for the societal groups who struggled to raise them. I came to love these women.

Tuesday evenings began with psychological warfare. Arriving for my first protective custody presentation, I found the guards brutal. Instead of greeting me with the gratitude I had come to enjoy in the general population, several of the guards were mean to me for wanting to work with violent offenders and rudely asked why I would bother wasting my time on "such pigs."

They assured me that I would never make a dent with this "group of murderers," because they were low-life criminals, sentenced to life and "goin' nowhere." Protective custody was a rough group and the guards treated me like the enemy.

The guards' attitude was seriously shocking and disturbing, but I didn't complain for fear that I would be seen as inadequate or too soft. Instead, I decided to win them over. It should only take a week or two, I thought. I would treat the guards to a strong dose of motivational kindness and before long . . .

Well, that didn't work. After several weeks of my kindness serving only to enhance their disgust, I decided to ignore the assholes and focus my attention on the women of Vanier.

There was one guard who was different, though. Respectful and amiable, Sheila was the only guard to ask how I was doing. She genuinely wondered if I could reach anyone.

"It's rough," I said. "But even prisoners need someone to care."

She replied, "You just might be doing well and doing good."

Sheila was becoming a friend and clued me in. The other guards were annoyed when I visited, she said, because it meant they had to give up their slack-off shift to babysit me at the "fishbowl" —their nickname for our glass-walled meeting room. I began to understand the animosity. Still, there was no apparent fix.

The guards made things awkward and even painful, but it was the kind of painful that motivated me to fight back. I wanted to prove to their nasty, cold hearts that I could reach some women. So, eventually, I left them to wallow in their hate while I spread a little love.

Working in protective custody, I was allowed ten attendees in my group. The women were delivered to me one at a time and patted down in my presence. (I think the guards actually enjoyed the ladies' embarrassment— or perhaps enjoyed something more.) I was locked into a glass-walled fish tank of a room with a collection of dangerous offenders, a stack of unstapled booklets and a big blue panic button that was hidden under the table where I sat. I was assured that upon pressing the panic button a guard would magically display and save the day. My day, should a threat or out of control prisoner present.

Hurray for Vanier.

Several guards surrounded "the tank," as it was called, and watched us. They sat themselves outside the tank to peer through the glass. By design, their very presence was intimidating as their straight backs, clenched jaws and intense eye contact conveyed distaste for both myself and the ladies— and an obvious preference that we not exist. Although it was comforting (for me) that they watched over us, it felt like I had a second audience—an unusually strange and hostile one. Then I realized the guards couldn't hear a damn thing. Inside the glass, we had privacy and we were good. So, I would smile at the guards from time to time hoping to impart confidence and assure them that we were all fine.

Miraculously, my new supply of patience arrived just in time for these forgotten and forsaken women. Their in-prison and out-of-prison love stories broke my heart. To be honest, it wasn't easy working with the women in protective custody. Most of them were either intellectually challenged or had deeply rooted psychological issues. But for years they looked forward to my visits, shared their struggles and searched for a reason to hope. After all, being locked up today with no hope for tomorrow is devastating. With expressionless faces, they called themselves lifers.

Talk about special ed. My years in protective custody were an education. They hammered home the idea of six degrees of separation and the real meaning of heartbreak. There but for the grace of God.

Meanwhile back in the general population, Destiny had served her sentence and was preparing to leave Vanier. On what would be my final Tuesday with Destiny, she called me aside after class and told me to take a seat in the laundry area. We needed some quiet time. Destiny had something private and important to say.

"I need to explain something," Destiny began with a seriousness that I had never seen before. "I care about you, and I need you to understand a few things. When we're in here, everyone is clean, and everyone is sober. We're not looking for our next fix. We're not gonna hit ya up for anything in here."

"But when we get out, we don't even trust ourselves. We turn a trick for a cabbie home. If we're lucky, we'll get home on a [blowjob]. So here it is: if you see me on the street, just run. Run away and ran away fast."

Destiny explained that when a woman leaves prison, she is given some donated clothing and the standard bus fare. The bus fare doesn't usually cover the ride home because she's often headed for a distant town. So, resourceful cabbies park outside the prison awaiting a sweet new release. When the happy cabbie scores a "fare," he'll take her anywhere she wants, in return for anything he wants.

Women prisoners find performing a homeward bound trick safer than hitchhiking. The message is clear: no one cares enough to provide even a safe ride home.

When women leave prison, they are fated to fail. Often, they're at risk within the first few hours. As long as the system remains the same, prisoners everywhere are victims of a cycle that encourages bad behaviour and puts all of us at risk.

My role is to create a safe and sacred space for women to share stories about their past and dreams for their future. For some of them, it's the first time they've ever received respect, caring or kindness. In working from a loving platform, my dream is to make a difference for women in pain. Together, we learn that there is a path to healing, which is critical to effecting change.

Destiny continued, "I mean it. I mean, you have a big heart and you trust everyone. But for your sake, we're not the same on the outside. We can't be trusted. None of us."

And then she added, without a trace of irony: "Trust me." And we hugged.

It was bittersweet saying goodbye to Destiny. Although our time together had ended, I never stopped appreciating her guidance and her belief in Tuesdays with Phyllis.

Seven years later, I found her again . . .

While at Vanier, Destiny had been working on her GED (General Education Diploma). Now living outside of Toronto, Destiny at age forty-six has managed to raise the money to return to school.

She is studying to become a registered veterinary technician, someone who works with animals to assist veterinary practitioners, public health officers and biomedical research scientists. Do I hear a mazel tov?!

I had the chutzpah to ask Destiny, clean, sober, and by now out of prison for seven years, how she felt about finding romance.

"Fuck the guys . . . no more guys, Phyllis."

"Yes, literally," I said, laughing as we both enjoyed the irony.

"What I appreciate now is sunshine and school," said a grateful Destiny, and then added, "Phyllis, you did so much for me. Keep helping us women."

My heart skipped a beat.

And there's more. A few years ago, Destiny reconnected with her mom, who now lives in Alberta. Visiting her mom, Destiny was surprised but ecstatic to learn that Mom, too, had "cleaned up her act."

"I am my mother's daughter, Phyllis, she taught me well. We both learned the hard way, but in the end, we both learned. She warned me about stuff but I wouldn't listen back then so I had to go down my own ugly path."

"Who cares, right? I'm on track now for a fabulous life!"

Despite Destiny's harsh beginning, she wanted me to know that there's good and bad everywhere—even a biker home. She endured some rottenness at the biker villa, but many of the folks there were kind.

"I just had some bad luck with the Hells . . . please don't give them a bad rap."

That's what we call forgiveness.

An extraordinary Destiny.

CHAPTER SIX

And then there were men

AFTER CREATING AN EXTENSIVE collection of presentations for Vanier, I thought it prudent to capitalize on my research and development efforts by adding more prisons to my schedule.

Coincidentally, just days later, I received a call from Dena Devine of OCI, the Ontario Correctional Institute for men in Brampton. Dena, who had heard about my popular gig at Vanier, wanted to bring me in.

After a brief telephone exchange, Dena said, "You'll love our guys. We're a treatment-centric facility. I'll explain when we meet."

"Monday at 1 p.m., Phyllis. See ya then."

Monday arrived and I met with a forty-something, four-foot-nine woman with wavy, shoulder-length black hair and a charming, intelligent smile. Dena personified control and respect. She knew how to deal with people for best results.

The dynamic interview lasted two and a half hours. Notwithstanding my commitment to Vanier, Dena had me right off the hop. She counselled me on the value of volunteerism and how to run a prison where the men knew exactly who was boss. Recognizing that Dena and I had some strong ethical commonalities, I thought we would get along just fine.

As part of the interview, Dena accompanied me on a detailed tour of the prison that included the intake process, a large gymnasium, wardrobe issuance, indoor and outdoor recreational facilities, sleeping quarters and an escape story. Pointing to the outdoor recreational facility, Dena proudly declared that in her twenty-three years with OCI there was only one escape attempt because barbed wire had not yet been installed. As I began to learn about the novel culture of OCI, I thought I could actually make a difference there.

Every prison has a distinct structure and unique culture. But more notable still is how each prison has its own personality and feel. Because OCI inmates apply (through their lawyers) to be accepted by and transferred to the facility, they take life seriously. These men realize they have been granted an opportunity for upgrade. Resulting from this realization, men exhibit confidence, take responsibility and try to earn favour with the staff. Not a bad thing.

Typically, a transfer to OCI means that the prisoner may not apply for early parole, nor shall they receive a reduced sentence for good behaviour, frequently earned in other prisons. In exchange for forfeiting these benefits, men receive life skills training, rehabilitative programs, specialized treatment, educational opportunities, work experience and decent food.

Within a few months of working with Dena, it became clear that when asked a favour, Dena would say "no." Eventually you'd get a "yes" provided that the favour was reasonable and benefitted her guys with a learning boost. Make no mistake, behind Dena's strict exterior, she could easily put down the lion and pick up the kitten.

In winter, my classroom got stinking hot. The men were shvitzing (sweating) and I was nearly fainting. Some guys were so hot they were dozing off, and by the end of class, everyone was smelly. I remember begging Dena to get the heating fixed but after weeks of unsuccessful adjustments, Dena insisted there was nothing more the superintendent could possibly do.

"That part of the building is unbalanced," she told me.

The following week, I was ecstatic to find my classroom set to a comfortable temperature. No explanation. It just happened. Today, Dena and I enjoy deep respect for one another, despite the odd peppery clash.

Pedophiles, drug salesmen, thieves and thugs all live together at the Ontario Correctional Institute. For some, it's just another day behind bars.

But for most, it's work. Sam, a repeat pedophile, says, "It's tough serving time at OCI." All inmates are required to take part in therapy, group sessions and honest peer-to-peer reviews. Sam was jailed and jailed again for sexually assaulting youngsters and so was attending the Sexual Offending Relapse Prevention Program.

OCI offers extensive correctional treatment, individual and group therapy sessions, and skill-enhancing initiatives. These treatments include: Alcoholics Anonymous, Cocaine Anonymous, Narcotics Anonymous, Gamblers Anonymous, General Education Diploma, wood-working classes, pool table for recreation, gymnasium activities, Sacred Circle (Indigenous Programming), musical band practice, Toastmasters meetings (public speaking) and countless programs for yoga, meditation and mindfulness. And of course, the Sexual Offending Relapse Prevention Program, which is said to actually work. (Since leaving OCI over a decade ago, Sam, for example, has not reoffended.)

Most of these opportunities set OCI apart from other provincial prisons.

You might expect that most correctional institutions are dedicated to education, counselling and rehabilitation. This is not the case. There is insufficient funding. In many institutions, prison budgets cover only guard and administrative staffing salaries. From my extensive experience in the prison system, (and of course my bias in favour of treatment), I believe that OCI is the only institution that offers inmates a sufficient opportunity to turn their lives around and become law abiding citizens.

Along with a safe and healing environment for the incarcerated, OCI also boasts zero tolerance for disrespect. Respect is meant to be reciprocal between prisoners and guards but while the guards receive a healthy dose of respect, alas, prisoners receive far less.

By the end of the interview with Dena, I had accepted a volunteer position at OCI and my training was booked. Dena, ended our talk with a smile and my instructions.

"After you've received training, you'll present every Monday at 1 p.m. When the count clears, that is." (Dena was referring to the head count carried out several times a day and meant to ensure that no man goes missing.)

"Let's call your sessions, Motivational Mondays. I like it!" Another brilliant smile.

"You'll be assigned to T-17 with Manuel Ferreira. Please send me your program schedule no later than Friday."

I didn't ask what a Manuel Ferreira was.

CHAPTER SEVEN

What's a Manuel Ferreira?

B Y FORTY, MANNY, a great-looking Portuguese career criminal, had spent twenty years in the Kingston Penitentiary before attending OCI. Manny was fond of boasting that he knew the most infamous Canadian serial killer-rapist, Paul Bernardo. Apparently, Manny and Paul had spent countless hours whispering through the air ducts while in solitary confinement. Manny said that even bad company was better than no company but made it clear that he was repulsed by serial killer Bernardo.

Manny had originally been incarcerated on charges of armed robbery and was serving time at the Kingston Penitentiary. During his incarceration, Manny's wife Angie was devoted to his needs, including medication and conjugal visits. Until the prison ruled that Angie could no longer visit Manny, insisting that she was handing over drugs, despite video surveillance disproving the accusation.

After a brief escape from the Kingston Penitentiary on his twenty-seventh birthday, Manny was surrounded by police. Upon capture, Manny was returned to corrections after having robbed a citizen of his car, at gunpoint. Emotionally distraught and mentally disturbed after being denied visits with his wife, Manny left Kingston to deliver a tragic letter to Angie asking her to divorce him and enjoy a life unburdened by a prison-husband. The police called it a suicide note and it easily could have been.

This unfortunate episode added an additional twelve years to a ten-year sentence under the worst maximum security conditions the Kingston Pen had to offer. Manny says the abuse and torture in Kingston has taken a toll medically, mentally, legally and physically.

After experiencing lockdown with both Bernardo and Milgaard, Manny clearly preferred the company of David Milgaard. You remember hiim. In 1969, David was a carefree teenage hippie just passing through Saskatoon when nursing assistant Gail Miller was raped and stabbed to death in a back alley. With sketchy forensics and unreliable witnesses, David was convicted of the crime and sentenced to life in prison. More than twenty years later, his case made national headlines when he became one of the most famous examples of wrongful conviction in Canadian history.

In preferring David over Paul, some might say that Manny is a good judge of character.

OCI is different than other prisons. Designated as a minimum-security prison, during the day inmates are free to walk the hallways unescorted as they navigate to counselling sessions or work assignments (cleaning, cooking, maintenance). Upon arrival at OCI for my first presentation, Manny met me at the control desk and escorted me to an assigned meeting room. Inmate Manny proudly explained that he was now a unit head and as such was tasked with keeping the boys in line. Additionally, Manny had volunteered to assist with my presentation requirements.

Before class, Manny would set up the seating, arrange the handouts and help with the projection equipment. Then he would prepare for class by positioning himself in his favourite seat—directly in front of me.

Shortly after I began at OCI, Manny decided that we should get better acquainted. He remained after class and, as we talked, I noted his gravelly deep voice. He was exceptionally well-spoken.

"I hear you do competitive public speaking," he began.

36

"Yes, since I was a kid. How about you?"

"We have Toastmasters here."

"Are you a member, Manny?"

"Yes, I've won several contests. It's awesome. Many of the guys find it a great release. A wonderful way to tell our stories and sort of like a support group."

And there it was. Manny and I had discovered a common interest, which gave birth to an everlasting friendship. Every week, Manny would sit himself in front of me to observe my pubic speaking skills and then stay for a chat after class. (After Manny left OCI, those after-class chats would become life-coaching sessions.)

Flatteringly, some of the men vied for my attention after class, so I rolled them into small group discussions. Of course, priority would still be given to someone who requested "alone time."

During Manny's tenure, it was amazing how easily he shared with me and even more amazing how easily I shared with him. I was comfortable with personal confidences and would tell Manny everything—including when I decided to leave my second husband. Manny got my whole divorce saga long before it went public, and so did the women of Vanier.

In the spirit of friendship, Manny told me about his past. He was also a victim of his childhood. He rarely spoke of his mother, except to describe her as quiet and very kind. But he often described his father as a frighteningly disturbed man who took his anger out on both Manny and his younger brother, Gabriel, known as Gabe.

"Me, well, I never had it too good . . ." Manny said, looking at his lap as he trailed off.

"My dad was a vicious guy. We used to hide when we heard him come home. He would drink—heavily. Never happy. Always looking to pick a fight or hurt someone. He had what you call out-of-control anger. Me and my brother lived in fear of getting battered," he said, lowering his voice to a whisper.

"Tell me more, Manny," I said, keeping a neutral tone.

"Late one night, Dad came home and I knew he'd been drinking. You could smell him down the hall. And he was stumbling and noisy as usual."

"Yes," I whispered.

Manny sat with me for a time looking pained, shamed and shaky. "Dad was an angry drunk. He had no love for no one. He always hid his gun. I never saw it. But that night, he came into our bedroom and, without speaking a word, ripped the sheets off our beds."

"Gabe and I were huddled together, wailing in the corner of the room. We were crying and screaming. We were hysterical. When Dad was drunk, he was vicious. But this time was different. He had his gun with him. I don't know if Gabe even saw the gun but I did."

"He began hollering. Swearing. Gabe and I were terrified. I knew something would go wrong. I just knew it. Gabriel, who was just eight at the time, screamed out in fear, 'Daddy, go to bed!'"

"A few seconds later, he shot Gabe. Right in front of me. One bullet, just one bullet, and Gabe was gone," Manny said as a single tear slid down his cheek.

Manny sat in silence for a while, just staring at the wall, reliving his most painful memory. We were both still and I was speechless.

Manny was ten when Gabe died. I don't know what happened to his mom, but the government paid for Gabe's funeral and Manny was put into foster care. As is often the case, foster parenting is worse than natural parenting. So, with continuing abuse and nowhere to go, Manny turned to heroin.

At twelve years of age, Manny became a drug addict and a very disturbed young man. He sought a life of crime, just petty crime at first and then robbery that escalated into armed robbery. Manny never imagined another way. He hated life and he hated people. Except for Angela, his first and only love.

Deeply in love, Manny and Angela married in their early twenties and meant every word of their vows. Through ten years of incarceration at the Kingston Penitentiary, followed by ten more, and an additional two years at OCI, Angela never stopped believing in Manny. She supported him emotionally, arranged whatever treatment she could from the outside and looked after the finances by working as a caregiver for the elderly. And she waited for Manny's release.

Studies show, and I decidedly agree, that when an inmate has someone on the outside rooting for them, believing in them, loving them, it counts. If an inmate has help after release, they have a much greater chance of getting their life back on track and reaching their healthy goals.

My unexpected confidant and I were deepening our relationship, and I didn't want our friendship to end with Manny's release. As Manny was leaving OCI, I asked what he was looking forward to the most.

"I'm looking forward to normal," he said looking up, imagining freedom. "You know, just being able to bend down and touch . . . even touch a blade of grass. For me, that's special."

Those hoped-for blades of grass would soon, literally, line Manny's path to a new life. But before he left prison, he taught me a lot about gratitude. Manny showed me how a "normal day" is a clear blessing. When the time came for Manny to leave, we were both saddened at the thought that our friendship might end.

For their own safety, volunteers are strictly forbidden from seeing former prisoners on the outside. Accordingly, we are not permitted to share our personal information. But I gave Manny my phone number and told him to keep in touch. I felt I had a responsibility to continue with him. It felt like my job.

And I could see the man he'd become. While serving his sentence at OCI, it became clear that Manny (formerly both a federal and provincial inmate), had transformed himself. He had learned values and earned the respect of everyone. I believe with all my heart that OCI provided Manny with an opportunity for change. I had faith that Inmate Manny would become a law-abiding citizen and a good friend. And I was right.

After Manny left OCI, we would meet for coffee every Monday on my way home from prison, at a Coffee Time in one of Toronto's seediest hoods. I may have felt safer in prison. But I fondly recall that with little money and much dignity, Manny always insisted on buying my coffee. Our friendship continued to thrive and, months later, Manny introduced me to his beautiful wife Angela. Two people believed in Manny now, but there was the one who had waited twenty-two years for his release.

When we met, I always had a hidden agenda. I would casually bring up Manny's job search efforts, modern marital challenges, family responsibilities, living arrangements, finances, temptation to use, transition back into society and the importance of getting his driver's licence reinstated. Sorry, Manny, it was all a setup!

As Manny was realizing freedom, he was considering ways to earn a respectable living. He had no idea where to begin. But, within six months, Manny's new found independence and natural creativity led to work as a gardener. He was beautifying some pretty respectable grounds. With his wonderful smile and personality, the jobs were growing and Manny was securing a good bit of yard work.

One day as Manny, Angela and I were sitting down for coffee, Manny announced that he was starting a business.

"Gee, Manny, I think you're already in business," I said.

"No, no. It's a business where I can hire people. I want to hire ex-cons. Give others a chance, at least get them started," he announced, beaming with pride.

Manny and Angela were both smiling with excitement. And I was bursting with pride as if Manny were my own son. I endorsed his idea, but I cautioned him to be very selective with his employee picks.

Manny was destined to become an outstanding, upstanding business-man. One who would provide countless opportunities for other ex-cons, affording them a chance to turn something pretty shitty into something good. Tellingly, Manny, the former heroin addict, had one critical rule for his employees: you do drugs, you go home.

As Manny began to acquire gardening projects, he also started to secure other work orders for snow removal, handyman gigs and house painting. Manny and his crew could handle it all with their collective skills and a determination to make their newly found freedom matter.

Today, Manny has a thriving business, employing only the finest. Manny's crew looks up to him as they learn that that life can be a bowl of ethics.

I couldn't be prouder of Citizen Manny.

My friendship with Manny underscored trust, respect and confidentiality. For me, it was a chance to redefine friendship and learn how an inclusive and non-judgmental platform could create an exceptional bond.

And working with Manny opened the gateway to personal discovery. I began to acknowledge my own painful childhood and humble beginnings. I came to understand that an unreasonable, demanding and abusive father had undoubtedly left scars. Years later, I was still dealing with troubling behaviour I needed to address.

During this time, and because of my work in the prison system, I reached out for professional counselling. Today, I continue to work on areas that need attention. I don't believe that seeking therapy is shameful, but needing therapy and not seeking it? Well, that might be.

Through therapy and personal examination, I understand now that opening myself up to those who have earned the right to hear my story is powerful. And that vulnerability encourages the kind of closeness that deepens a relationship.

Which leads us to my vulnerabilities.

CHAPTER EIGHT

Humble beginnings

W HY WOULD TWO PEOPLE MARRY who were not in love and had nothing in common? Meet my parents! They rushed down the aisle in the hopes of children, but Mom and Dad never paused to discuss how those children would be raised or what marriage might imply. After all, when marriage has an "urgent" sticker, why bother with details? With Gertrude well into her thirties and Calvin full on forty, the only motivator was "tick tock."

Gertrude was a beautiful, vivacious, loving gal who was heavy on personality and light on worldliness and intelligence. But, hey, she did well with her stunning good looks, warm ways and social talents. People called her "corsage receiving," as she was quite popular with the gentlemen. Although Mom wanted to settle down and raise children, she couldn't seem to narrow down the field. Until one day she realized that her friends and colleagues were married while she was still selling shoes at Eaton's. She was on course to becoming an old maid.

Calvin was a rather brilliant fellow with strong good looks, a painfully introverted personality and a dash of anger. Okay, make that a shitload of anger. According to family lore, Calvin was one credit short of a medical degree when his father died. Traumatized by the loss, and forced to carry on the family schmatta (clothing) business, Calvin never completed his medical training.

Eventually, Calvin became a frustrated, antisocial, low-income earning life insurance salesman. This epic fail may well have been a major contributor to Calvin's angry outbursts and passive-aggressive behaviour.

Dad went to war and met Mom on his return. Problems began the very day they wed. Honeymooning at Niagara Falls, it quickly became apparent that they agreed on nothing—except making babies. Each party had chosen poorly, simply because a Jewish mate was more valuable than a compatible one. The marriage was dysfunctional and, with their antiquated thinking, divorce was not an option.

Foolishly, Gertrude and Calvin had never discussed their approach to religion or how radical an approach to Judaism would be administered by Dad and tolerated by Mom. My father was an Orthodox Jew, complete with yarmulke (skull cap) and tallit (prayer shawl). He believed that if you were not Jewish, you were not okay. Some of Dad's family had narrowly escaped the Holocaust, which contributed to my father's racial intolerance.

As the infamous horrors of Hitler's Nazis became known, Dad collected testimonials to the hatred of Jews, widely known as anti-Semitism. Although we understood that his mission was to enlighten, his audience was restricted to immediate family and his delivery left much to be desired.

My Mom Gertrude was a bit of a closet shiksa (Yiddish for a non-Jewish girl or woman). Well entrenched in Judaism, Gertrude still snuck us out the back door for bacon and eggs. Extra bacon, extra crispy.

After the wedding bells stopped, the silence was filled with the sound of my parents' arguments. Most kids have trouble believing their parents ever got naked. In our case, it was even less believable, since Mom and Dad never stopped fighting long enough to enjoy dinner. Nonetheless, a girl (me) and a boy (my brother Allan) were born to Calvin and Gertrude Blitzstein.

We didn't have a happy childhood. We never did the zoo thing. Nor were there any family picnics or even restaurant outings (restaurants aren't kosher, after all). Books were seen as toys and toys were meant for others.

I had an overzealous, addictive need to make outside friends. At five years of age, I gave my friend Judy's mother hell when she wouldn't let Judy outside to play. I felt she had no right to keep Judy away from me. For me, friendship was everything. (And nothing has changed.)

At home, adherence to religion and punishment for noncompliance was a way of life, but Calvin's physical abuse was chiefly directed at me. (Allan, who ran faster than Dad, would lock himself in the bathroom to escape.) I was treated severely. Without hesitation, I was strapped and badly beaten for bringing home a friend who wasn't Jewish or a report card that wasn't stellar.

The last time my dad beat me it left visible scars. I recall looking up at him thinking: You're not mad at me, Daddy, you're angry with yourself. My dad was not only hurting me as a result of his anger, he was hurting me to release it. I was what's called the "scapegoat child."

As a kid, I was terrified, so I challenged myself to live a life that was over the top but under my parent's radar. I learned that friends were supportive and parents were dangerous. I discovered that life began outside the home, where I could brush up against the normalcy of others. I indulged in exaggerated makeup, big hair and age-inappropriate clothing. I used provocative language and loved the company of boys (Jewish or not). I was determined to have fun and pray later.

As a kid, I never thought of my childhood as abusive or even unusual. I assumed a beat down was part of an ordinary day for all us kids. I never spoke of it, nor did I focus on it. But, years later, when I began my work in the prison system, my childhood abuse came crashing into awareness. Hearing the emotional and heartbreaking accounts of the men and women who were battered as children triggered my own childhood memories; the hostility and harshness that accompanied Calvin's definition of wrong. These memories demanded I look within and develop a deeper sense of empathy and compassion for others.

Today, I look back on my childhood without regret nor remorse. A parent's behaviour is a chance for learning and although Dad was quite a crazy bastard, he actually loved his children. On some unfounded level, he believed that only by delivering severe punishment would we learn to be good people. We all know this is not a prescription for raising kids, but with a hint of love in Dad's radical approach to child rearing, it sort of worked.

Dad's religious code made him a kind of ethical guru. So, baked into our DNA was a demand for truth and transparency, honouring our word, taking responsibility, high-level professionalism and respect for mankind.

Still, he did me damage. It wasn't until my work in the prisons that I began to admit that I didn't have a loving home. I had parents who didn't love one another, didn't even like one another, and were barely hanging on. My dad accessed his deepest hostility, resentment and anger and then applied it liberally as a homemade recipe for family living.

We never celebrated, never travelled and my parents had absolutely no friends. My mother began distancing herself from other family as well. Although we had some really sweet cousins, they were never a part of our lives. Embarrassment, jealousy and shame breed such unfavourable outcomes.

At age sixty, after discovering my aunt had passed away, I dared to reconnect with family. I hadn't seen most of my cousins since childhood, but I attended Auntie Esther's shiva, the week-long Jewish mourning period that begins immediately after burial. I'm glad I did. Today, while it took time and effort, my cousins and I enjoy a meaningful relationship.

In my research into childhood trauma, I've learned a lot from the work of Dr. Gabor Maté, a renowned addiction and behavioural specialist. The son of a Jewish family in Hungary during World War II, Maté's maternal grandparents were killed at Auschwitz, and his father was forced into Nazi labour camps. Immigrating to Canada after the war, Maté became a doctor and found his niche with Vancouver's East Side drug addicts.

Maté teaches addiction counsellors worldwide about the research and findings on Adverse Childhood Experiences (ACE). These studies show that when childhood trauma is experienced, sometimes caused unwittingly by loving parents, it paves the way for unhappy adults who may suffer addiction, mental health issues or the inability to forge healthy relationships.

ACE research supports Maté's theory that, as the number of negative physical, sexual or emotional experiences increase, so do the levels of depression, alcoholism, promiscuity and suicide attempts later in life.

When friends or colleagues speak of historic family picnics or loving parents, I can't relate. I envy the woman who speaks of her mom as her best friend; the mom who passed away and is deeply missed years later. My mother spent her life crying, depressed, lonely and actually a bit nutty. When Dad got angry, Mom got scared. She seemed not to have the wherewithal or desire to protect me when violence erupted. Along with bacon, Valium was Mom's saviour.

At seventy-two, Mom finally left Dad, enrolled at the University of Toronto as a mature student and became self-sufficient. And, alas, self-absorbed. Not that I blame her much. It was simply impossible for us to form that long overdue bond. But Mom was finally happy and that was good. I forgave both of my parents long before forgiveness was a thing.

Did any of this have an effect on me? Of course it did. I felt that I was not enough. But I later discovered that being different is a vulnerability. And vulnerability is often the birthplace of creativity, innovation and change. Today, as a motivational speaker, I've been blessed with a role in which being different is applauded.

During my Trust Yourself, Trust Others presentation, I begin: "Today, I want to share something special with you. I want you to know that I love myself."

A sea of stunned faces look back at me. How can someone say a thing like that? The naked truth is that we must all learn to love ourselves, our core values and what we stand for. In short, we must love and feel love-worthy.

I can tell you personally, from the hundreds of stories my audiences—in and out of prison—have shared with me over the years, there has never been a sad story that didn't begin with acute childhood pain or trauma. And some of it begins in the womb.

If childhood has had an adverse effect upon you, perhaps as a result of bullying or other traumatic experiences, your self-worth may rise and fall according to what other people think. You may find yourself looking for external affirmations rather than looking within. If you feel that way, you're not alone. But we will challenge this mindset and find new ways of moving forward in these chapters.

Hurt people holler, but we can learn to holler in a positive way. Don't look for reasons to take yourself out of the game. Look for reasons to stay—and to thrive. Respect yourself. Applaud yourself. And then celebrate your differences.

You deserve to love yourself wholeheartedly. And enjoy a life of passion.

CHAPTER NINE

Publicly speaking

BECAUSE DAD WAS AN awkward and introverted fellow, he vowed that his daughter would exemplify a powerful life force. From the age of twelve, I was forced to memorize *Reader's Digest* articles, modify them somewhat, and compete in every public speaking contest this side of Maniac River.

I fought it. I won plenty of contests, but I fought it.

How could I know that those public speaking gigs would become my lifeline and most cherished tool? I often wonder how I might have fared had I not been forced into competitive speaking. It explains a lot.

It is also notable that because I grew up with a basic "needs only" survival kit, I developed a deep and lasting empathy for those who are disenfranchised, marginalized, isolated or in any sort of trouble. I was riveted by different and difficult people with a view to understanding their plight and fighting their fight. I fantasized about becoming Barbara Walters or some other "60 Minutes" journalist, so I could give these people a boost and a platform.

While in high school, in addition to my public speaking, there were other stage performances. In defiance, I became the "dancing queen." A full blown, light up the stage, go-go dancer. I was speaking publicly by day and dancing publicly by night in Toronto's hippie haven—Yorkville Village. I achieved an enormous measure of confidence both on and off the stage. Especially, on stage!

At the same time, home life became increasingly unpleasant and, at times, even frightening. Dad continued to apply his radical approach to parenting while Mom, on her better days, tried to hold love-ins. They argued, sometimes fiercely, and everyone lost.

Violent behaviour in a family setting is abuse. Understanding now what anger is all about, it has become abundantly clear why dad beat me. My father was an angry bastard who used excessive rage and radical Judaism to control our home. He also gave me first hand experience of what it's like to live in captivity—something that helped in my work with prisoners later—but that story deserves its own chapter.

CHAPTER TEN

You go, girl!

MY TEENS BEGAN WITHOUT INCIDENT, but they ended with me confined for a year to a dark basement with boarded windows buttressed with barbed wire.

My troubles began when I spotted Paul at the local pizza joint. At fifteen, he had a strong build, Elvis-style hair and a passionate personality. He loved music and he loved to dance. What more could a girl want?

Knowing my father would beat me for less, I was not about to bring Paul home to meet the folks. My new guy was rooted in Catholicism and wore a highly polished gold cross rather than a yarmulke.

Only Lynda (the same friend who, years later, would drag me to see Oprah) knew about Paul. He is still her most entertaining high-school memory. Lynda and I met in Mr. Coristine's social studies class in Grade Nine. For us, that class was about getting to know one another, the hidden wonders of a neighbourhood hangout and an intimate boyfriend story exchange that I entitled, "How to Lose Your Virginity and Gain a Boyfriend."

Hottie Paul, now officially my steady by virtue of a charming but fake black diamond ring, had raging hormones and didn't much care for homework. Our secret teen love brought sex and sexual desire to a whole other level of magic. And I liked it.

50

My parents were not into sex education. In fact, they never spoke of sex. I imagine their thinking was that if you don't talk about it, it won't happen. Consequently, at the age of fifteen, I had little understanding of either conception or contraception. It seemed reasonable to me that after making love, having a shower with Paul was a great way to avoid making a baby. I still wonder how I managed to avoid teen pregnancy. A solid for God.

The most impressive thing about Paul, besides his noticeable good looks and a driver's licence, was his cool teen job. (This also turned out to be his grownup job.) Paul was a career DJ and, in those days, all good DJs worked with a go-go dancing duo. Enter stage left, Paul's girlfriend Phyllis (me) and stage right, her gorgeous friend Loretta Petrowski.

The best thing about Loretta, besides her enviable figure, thick black hair, dusky skin tone and natural beauty, was that she could sew. Loretta quickly created our go-go dancing costumes from matching turquoise bellbottom pants, skimpy white bikini bra-like tops and a trunk load of white fringe. To finish the look, we each purchased a pair of white go-go boots that appeared to be made for us and made for dancing. Loretta and I were outrageously confident and ready to take on the world of teen dance. Our plan was to heighten the awareness of dance music globally and to be known by teens everywhere. Hell, we would even end up on American Bandstand.

Most evenings, immediately after Calvin and Gertrude were comfortably tucked into their tiny twin beds, it was game on. I would silently crawl onto the countertop under the window of my basement bedroom. The opening was just wide enough to fit my teenage ass if I sucked in my tummy and twisted my waist. It was through this handy window that I snuck my girlfriends in to party at night and squirrelled myself out to hitchhike down to Yorkville.

Yorkville, the coolest area of Toronto, was a drug-infested, free sex, come-out-of-whatever-closet-you-want mecca. It was where I landed a thrice-weekly gig at Boris's Discotheque, complete with a shiny silver cage and psychedelic strobe lights that illuminated the stage. The chunky silver braces on my teeth didn't exactly enhance the look, but I learned that if I didn't smile too widely, I could still look hot. I had saved up just enough money to buy makeup and a can of extra hard, extra hold, number nine hair spray. I was ecstatic. It didn't matter that I was dancing all night and sleeping all day in school. I loved the electricity of the stage. You know, like Dad taught me.

Oh, the excitement of a secret life among the love child set. After dancing the evening away, I would watch them make out in their group-style love-ins and counsel them on addiction. Against all odds, I was totally disinterested in trying out their hippie-style psychedelic drugs or their sex free-for-alls. I just wanted to be there, disco dance, chat a bit and go home. After all, I had school the next day.

But then. . . .

It was the wee hours of the morning. I had just hitchhiked home from Yorkville, exhausted and exhilarated from dancing. As always, I started to climb back into the house through the small basement window, expecting to cozy up in bed and catch a nap before school. I was straddling the window ledge when I saw them. My parents were sitting in my bedroom. Side by side. In complete darkness. Creepy.

How did I get caught?

Our tiny bungalow sided onto a dirt path where our neighbour's son, Harvey Weinberg, was walking his dog. As I was backing out of the window earlier, Harvey spotted my ass protruding through the westerly brick wall. Harvey was intellectually challenged and maybe he found the sight strangely terrifying because he ran home and told his mom who, without hesitation, called mine.

My parents, checking, found my empty bed with a pillow tucked under the covers masquerading as me. (Also, a two-by-two-foot window was lying conspicuously on the freshly mowed lawn. I think the window might have been a giveaway.)

And now, here were my parents, perched on their black bridge chairs, looking eerily like they were sitting shiva. They were motionless. The only thing visible were the whites of their eyes, dangerously aglow. I began to panic.

My first thought was to yank my leg off the counter, back out of the window and run like hell. But my next thought was: Where the hell would you go? Maybe I could pass out on the window ledge? With life now a horror flick, I instinctively knew that my teen fun was at an end.

I slid my body into the room and faced a punishment that no kid should ever know. It wasn't a rant. It wasn't even a conversation. It was a slow descent into hell. Gertrude would now drive me directly to and from school. (This penalty was nasty enough because, at fifty, Mom had secretively earned a driver's licence but could never really drive well.) And there were weeks when I remained in lockup, simply because Mom wasn't up to the task.

To secure my captivity, Calvin installed prison-style barbed wire and black wooden boards across every basement window. His ambition was to fully darken my space and frighten me into best behaviour.

But there was more to come. During my emotional rambling confession, I revealed that I had met someone. Big mistake. My mother hastily retrieved my Not-a-Virgin-Anymore Diary and using her garden shears, forced open the lock. Even back then I could describe an event in full living colour. So, with all my detailed sexcapades revealed, Calvin violently forced me into providing Paul's phone number by threatening his demise.

Calvin contacted Paul before I could render a father-on-the-loose alert. He threatened Paul physically, screaming that he must never again come near me. Naturally, I wasn't privy to this conversation, but on one of our school joyrides, my mother confided that Paul had threatened to "kill himself" on the family driveway. Not that there was any real benefit from this proclamation of love, but in those days his response kept me going. Actually, it still feels good to this day.

My cherished go-go dancing was over. All makeup and hairspray provisions were confiscated, and I was not permitted to kiss Paul goodbye.

I cried myself to sleep for weeks until I began to accept that there was no path out of this. I resorted to dreaming about yesterday when hope was high, excitement was experiential and happiness was within reach. Most days, I was allowed to attend school. Otherwise, I was confined to the basement for a non-negotiable period of twelve months. A solid year of confinement and isolation with no sign of civilization or early parole. I was on a basic meal plan with no access to a telephone, television or typewriter. Even the lightbulbs were removed to ensure darkness.

It was a horrific situation. My father told me: "If I ever hear you so much as speak with this shaygitz (non-Jewish male person) again, I will sit shiva for you." And he closed with: "For me, you won't exist." I had shamed a family who insisted upon exclusivity.

Life in our toxic home as I was held hostage in a small, dark, restricted space was depressive and morbid. And it came at a price. To this day, unless I'm deeply involved in a work-related project or a telephone call, I have great difficulty when left alone, even for short periods of time. This has many challenges that I continue to work on today.

As I look back on serving that one-year term of solitary confinement however, I derive purpose. It provided me with sharp and meaningful insight. Albeit more humane than prison life, my experience prepared me to identify with the challenges and fears faced by the incarcerated souls who touch my heart. It provided me with an increased capacity for empathy and it emboldened me to speak up in defence of others. And yes, my glass is always half full.

Since childhood, I have demonstrated a pattern of calculated risk-taking. While working with prisoners involves a different kind of risk than hitchhiking or go-go dancing, it also carries a far greater and more precious reward.

CHAPTER ELEVEN

Mitchell and mental health

EOPLE ARE GENUINELY curious about my work in the prison system. "Aren't you nervous working in a prison? Isn't it scary? Don't you fear for your life?"

I smile and say, "I feel safer in prison than I do in a shopping mall. It's simple. I love my guys and they love me back. Why would anyone hurt me? I help these guys. Often, I'm the only person who provides a safe space, unconditional respect and a reason for hope."

But I do have a few rules for my audience and these rules are reinforced every week. This is my narrative:

Confidentiality:

"Good afternoon, everyone. For those of you who are new, my name is Phyllis. Thank you for allowing me into your home. I believe that I am on sacred ground when I am here with you. My goal is to create a safe space for everyone to share their thoughts without fear of their disclosures ever leaving this room. Please share freely today.

"Agreed?"

All heads nod.

Togetherness:

"Together we create a bond of friendship, of trust and of love. Regarding friendship, I'm your friend, too, but I'm only here once a week. When I leave, I ask that you be kind to one another. For me, this group forms a village, a village culture that has respect and kindness at its core.

"Agreed?"

All heads nod.

Respect:

"Together we learn and together we exude respect. I have a zero tolerance for anyone who shows a lack of respect.

"Your respect for me is deeply appreciated. But I ask that when one of our guys has the courage to speak, it, too, is revered. We show everyone 100 percent respect. And you will thank me. You will thank me when it's your turn to speak."

They know the drill. They're already nodding.

"So, if I hear laughter or whispering or if you so much as roll your eyes when a friend is speaking, I will invite you to leave.

"Agreed?"

All heads nod and we begin.

If I remove anyone from my class for disruptive behaviour, they are at risk of losing their placement at OCI. This would mean that they could be transferred to a high security prison to serve out their remaining time. No one wants that.

I'm frequently asked if my work actually makes a difference. I have no metrics, nor do I have reliable markers. But I believe that much of my stuff sticks. My prison friendships seem to validate this belief. Call it intuition. You just know when something feels right.

I've seen it work. And heartbreakingly, I've seen it fail to reach some who desperately needed it.

Canada's prisons are failing the mentally ill and efforts to deliver medical care to these prisoners is unreliable at best. An overburdened and overcrowded prison system struggles to effectively support inmates with mental health challenges.

Because of the extensive treatment, counselling and educational sessions offered at OCI, classroom and meeting spaces sort of resemble what one might see in a public-school setting, except that rooms vary in size, are at a premium and assigned to facilitators according to session requirements. A few meeting rooms accommodate computers that are placed around the perimeter of the room. OCI computers have no access to internet or external communication to ensure that there are no pornography or people opportunities (like email or social media). Each room has a wooden door with a large window and guards patrolling the hallways. During class sessions the doors remain unlocked and there is no blue panic button at OCI.

Over the last decade, my audience has grown from a dozen to a hundred, fluctuating at times depending upon intake and conflicting programming. When I began volunteering at OCI, I was assigned a small room, a dozen men and a precise topic. I was asked to teach resume writing and job search techniques. Feeling I could maximize my time by delivering life skills, (after begging Miss Devine) I was granted the life skills program and assigned a larger meeting room. And although our meeting room had floor to ceiling windows where the outdoor yard was in plain view, the men were focused on me. These men recognized that their second chance was important to them and so was my time.

Notably, I've had only one behavioural incident; it occurred well into my second year.

When speaking publicly, I prefer a theatre-style format. This setup accommodates row seating and folding chairs (no tables). For safety purposes with a prison audience, I feel it's critical that no one is seated behind me. And eye contact with the men is essential for building trust and forming connections. Of course, eye contact is impossible when an inmate is sleeping, which can happen when using methadone to wean off opioid street drugs. But hey, I get it.

At OCI, the "all aboard" head count begins at noon, the medication cart arrives shortly after and, after popping their pills, the men file into my auditorium. The inmates usually take their seats and speak quietly among themselves while awaiting the lesson.

They were settling in when I noticed a new young inmate enter the room. He sauntered in slowly, dragging his feet and seemingly oblivious to protocol. Usually new attendees walk in, check out what others are doing and follow suit. But not this guy. He walked gingerly over to the seating area, grabbed a chair and hauled it away to the back of the room. And there he sat, separated from the group and leaning his chair against the back wall. He began to balance on the back legs of his chair, leaving the front legs suspended.

Calmly, I walked over to him and in a casual tone, said, "Hi, I'm Phyllis. What's your name?"

An inaudible mumble.

I repeated my question more loudly so the others could hear.

No answer.

By this time, everyone was watching—about forty men.

One more try. "Please bring your chair back into the seating area so we can begin." And I walked to the front like we were good.

He remained motionless and the room became tense.

I returned to the young inmate taking a position directly in front of him and, in a soft and respectful tone, said, "I'm sorry, we can't begin until—"

Suddenly, he lunged from his seat, turned to grip his chair and, spinning, violently thrust it at the wall. The chair bounced off the wall, narrowly missing my head. A nanosecond passed. I was frightened. Everything is a weapon. His face was on fire. With squinting eyes and reddened skin, he jerked around and violently propelled the chair towards me.

I was shaking, the blood rushing from my head, and feeling faint with nowhere to sit.

As I was losing focus, five men surrounded me and escorted me to a chair. Five other men ran to my offender, lifted him up and carried him outside the auditorium. I learned later that while three men surrounded him, two went in search of the guards.

Had there been a panic button, I would have invoked it that day. Prison guards are never present in session rooms, nor are they posted outside the door. They continuously walk the halls. But inmates are on the alert for tense situations and a high value is placed on taking responsibility for self and others who occasionally fall out of line. They stepped up generously that day. The men who removed the young inmate had handed him over to guards and quietly re-entered the room. Meanwhile, the remaining men were asking how I was feeling and apologizing on behalf of OCI. I deeply appreciated their concern and protection. It was marvelous, feeling the love.

My lesson that day was forgiveness. Since my heart was still beating rather anxiously, I began the lesson slowly and with no introductory chat. We had had enough rules for one day. But I used the incident as a teaching moment to commend the leader who had acted so quickly, and I acknowledged a feeling of oneness in the room.

Interrupting my lesson, Dena Devine appeared at the door and asked to meet with me after class. Somehow, I got through the lesson, packed up and proceeded to the executive offices. When I arrived, the troublemaker (whose name, I learned, was Mitchell), was seated in the room with Dena, a security guard and a psychologist. Dena conducted the meeting and each of us had a chance to speak, or shall I say, to lecture Mitchell. It was not a fun event.

Finally, Dena turned to me and said, "Phyllis, is there anything you'd like to add?"

That was like asking a fully dilated birthing mom if she still wanted to deliver the baby. Yes, I had something to add, and everyone would listen up.

I paused to collect myself and began.

"Mitchell, you would have no idea who I am, but I'm a volunteer at OCI. I've been here for a couple of years now, and this is my thing. It's a very important part of my life. I come here every Monday with the hope that I can talk to men like you and help them. But, Mitchell, you never gave me a chance. You never allowed me to help you or even speak with you."

"Do you think that's fair?"

The room fell silent. Mitchell was not making eye contact with anyone. He was staring down at his knees. And I'm thinking: give him time.

I had no idea how to reach Mitchell, but I knew I must try.

"Mitchell, would you please allow me another chance? A chance to work with you. I don't want you to be upset over today. But I do want to understand you better and have you understand me."

The room was so quiet I could hear my heartbeat.

"I have a favour to ask of you, Mitchell. I want you to return to my class on Monday and sit with the rest of us. I want to earn your trust. Could you do that for me?"

The crowded office was still; all eyes fixed on me. I'm an extrovert. I love this.

Appearing shameful, Mitchell faced me for the first time and whispered, "Yes, Ma'am."

And everyone looked at me like I just scored a bank heist.

Moments seemed to pass until Dena said, "Mitchell, do you have anything more to say to Phyllis?"

In the softest voice possible, Mitchell said, "I'm sorry, Miss. See you Monday."

Mitchell was escorted back to his cell and I was done. I mean emotionally, just done.

When an inmate exhibits violent behaviour at OCI, most often he's transferred to a high security prison. In this case it was decided that because Mitchell was a new intake and all things considered, he would be given another chance.

Not unlike other prisons, inmates at OCI may suffer with cognitive deficiencies, emotional issues or mental illness. Mitchell's behaviour was consistent with emotional issues and perhaps even mental illness. For reasons of privacy, I am not privy to prisoners' medical status but am keenly aware that anger is associated with many mental health conditions, including: antisocial personality disorder. And that calls for compassion.

Months later, I learned that Mitchell's dad was serving time for second degree murder and sentenced to life in a federal penitentiary—they never spoke. Mom had money, though. Apparently, she was good at robbing shops without getting caught. Mitchell's mother visited her boy every month like clockwork and was dedicated to dropping off bucks for canteen. I guess we do what we can.

As promised, Mitchell returned to class the following Monday and although he was seated with the rest of the group, he sat motionless and seemingly disoriented during the entire session. He left without so much as a backward glance.

Convicted felons who are mentally ill deserve the same human rights as anyone. Often, the mentally challenged inmate shouldn't be there in the first place and truly belongs with our health care professionals.

So why are so many mentally challenged people incarcerated?

Developmental issues associated with offending such as absentee parents, poverty, substance abuse at home, physical or emotional abuse are often found to be at the core of severe mental illness. Offenders are usually incarcerated rather than treated for their issues.

Symptoms of mental illness are often the very cause of criminal behaviour. Delusional fear and paranoia or the ill-tempered and extravagant ideation experienced in a manic episode are mental states which elicit aggressive behaviour. Sometimes police will recognize a mental health issue and call for professionals. But if the offence is serious, it will likely result in criminal charges regardless.

Many of the inmates I work with experience this; mental health challenges leading to criminal behaviour and, eventually, prison.

Incarceration could mean being locked away without sufficient mental health treatment. And the wait to see a therapist is long and agonizing.

Do we want these people on the streets, leaving us vulnerable? Heck, no.

Could we do better? Of course, we can and we must.

More must be done to separate the mentally ill from the criminally ill, even when it crosses over. But successful outcomes take dollars. More money must be invested in our mental health system. Period. Not only where it pertains to mental health that leads to criminal behaviour, but for mental health in general.

I'm not an expert in the field of mental illness. But countless stories shared with me would suggest that the wait for mental health support is shocking, and the duration of treatment, minimal. Insufficient treatment may lead to hopelessness. And hopelessness never has a happy ending.

Additionally, an inmate may have difficulty obtaining the pharmaceutical drug treatment that had met their mental illness challenges on the outside. In the prison system, mentally ill prisoners may be taken off the medication prescribed by their doctor and given a more affordable alternative. When this occurs, their hope and health can be diminished. The trauma and fear of prison, combined with this drug shakeup, can have a disastrous outcome.

It's shameful.

Isolation and loneliness are immense contributors to mental illness, substance abuse and a shortened life expectancy. Best outcomes occur when a mentally ill patient has an advocate. Someone who loves them, or at least cares. Have you ever seen chronic homelessness? It personifies mental illness on the periphery of society. We must take greater care of our marginalized people.

Mitchell never returned to my sessions, but he was my greatest teacher of humility. This episode revealed that although I might shine a light for someone, they won't necessarily follow it. It was extremely painful for me not to have reached Mitchell, and I struggle to accept that I lost a lost soul.

CHAPTER TWELVE

The legend of Cowboy Gord

WHEN GORD BOYD strolled into class, he seated himself in the back row. He was so knockout splendid that I stared at him in disbelief. Gord's thick, slick, shiny black hair rested softly on his neck and, with his tall athletic build, Gord was a vision. He was attractive alright, and with him in the room it felt more like a movie set than a prison.

At fifty-five, Gord was a lone cowboy, very sexy with a seductive voice. The guy was fascinating. I couldn't help myself. I have always loved John Wayne. Thinking about him was like birthday cake at a Weight Watchers lunch—forbidden, but tempting. Worse, he seemed to know that I found him attractive. And that was awkward.

What do we do with awkward? Why, we get to know it, of course.

About a month later, an opportunity presented itself. It was Anger Management day, and I was telling the guys about Tony, a scary tough guy I had words with at Maplehurst Correctional Complex (more about that later).

From the back of the room I heard, "You work at Maplehurst?" Gord asked, leaning into the crowd with disbelief.

"Yes," I responded enthusiastically, "Why do you ask?"

"You don't seem like a Maplehurst gal. That's all," he replied provocatively.

"Interesting, Gord," I answered and continued the lesson.

Damn, why did I use his name? I don't know most of their names, I thought.

A few minutes later, I stopped mid-sentence, turned to Gord and said, "Could we chat for a while after class today, Gord?"

There's my chutzpah again.

"Sure," he said slowly, in that low voice.

I admit that I was a wee bit delighted. Frankly, it was old fashioned excitement with a cherry on top. Not that it's unusual to speak with a guy after class, but it was Gord. After weeks of staring at one another, I had nailed him for a chat. Maybe I was sweet on him, but chatting's good, right? Okay, maybe I was between marriages but, in general, I prefer a guy not in prison.

When Gord sat down, my mind played tricks. His orange jumpsuit and runners became a crisp white shirt, fashionably torn blue jeans and flat-polished black boots. (Give me a break. At least he was dressed.)

As we spoke, I was drawn to Gord's large, dark eyes. They smiled like they had a secret and left me lightheaded. Add to this a mouth that sort of twisted to accommodate the eyes, and the package was brimming with bad behaviour and good sexuality.

Chatting freely about his life, it was amazing how quickly the conversation flowed. Gord, an engaging and animated storyteller, shared some amusing tales about his life as a drug dealer. He admitted that OCI was a decent place to hang but much too soft.

"So you prefer Maplehurst?" I asked sarcastically.

"Well, I'm not sure. I was just transferred from Maplehurst."

"What am I hearing, Gord?"

"Maplehurst is no place to live," I emphasized. "Give us a chance, my friend."

Maplehurst—the Hurst—is a death trap. It's where two guys hold your head in the toilet and walk away calling it "potty-time." The guards never discover who did it and the poor bastard is toast. Constantly in lockdown, even a missing shower tile is a weapon at Maplehurst.

"Nah, it's boring here. All these mandatory classes. The soft guys . . . not for me."

The "soft guys" was a reference to sex offenders and pedophiles. For some reason, OCI is noted for an abundance of soft guys who are handpicked for rehabilitation.

"Gord, how much is left on the ticket?"

"Ten months," he said, smiling like he was going somewhere exceptional.

"Give OCI time. Stick with me. Take these classes a while longer. Let's see how you feel in a bit." I was begging.

"Maybe," he said, rubbing his chin and considering his options. "But where I do time don't matter. I get out, reoffend, come back. Simple." And with that he smiled broadly and shrugged his shoulders as if to say: What's the difference?

"That will change, Gord."

"Nah, I'm a lifer, serious heroine junkie. Soon as I get outta here, I'll do a lift, shoot up, get caught, do time." He shrugged his shoulders again, this time tilting his beautiful head.

"Let's work together, Gord. A few adjustments could save your life." My high energy was throttling up. Admittedly, it's firmly engaged most days. "You have so much going on. Look at you. An awesome guy."

"Whoa girl, you're close to admitting you're human," he said excitedly. I ignored him.

"Life doesn't need to be this way, Gord. There's so much more for you. C'mon buddy," I exclaimed, trying to be cool. "Look, I've got this, Gord. I've helped so many others. Guys like you. Together, we'll develop a strategy for you to stay clean and out of trouble."

I was begging again and it was pathetic.

"Do you have kids, Gord?" I probed, hoping for motivation.

"Nah, nothin' like that. Never stayed with a woman long enough," he said, beaming, as if to say he had so many secrets my hair would frizz.

And I'm thinking: Oy, this is not for me. As if.

But it was so much fun.

"Gord, we can do this. I'll see you next week, my friend."

He stood, gave me that seductive, mysterious smile and walked out.

I had told Gord that for every reason he found to use drugs, there was a far greater reason not to. In the weeks that followed, we explored every potential for bringing goodness into his life. I urged him to stay clean and maintain a clear mind for decisions that would be life-altering.

But I was competing with historical pain and an unwavering risk taker. Like many other Gords, this man had frequent flyer parents. An only child, Gord was constantly tossed from aunt to aunt when one or both of his parents did time. Mostly small amounts of time but enough to destroy a kid.

By age thirteen, Dad was doing a longer stint. And his mom politely asked if Gord would mind leaving home, explaining that she was no longer up for parenting. Mom was in and out of prison so often that Gord never knew if he was coming home to a cooked meal or an overnight stay with Aunt Maryanne. And so, at thirteen years young, Gord was homeless. He sometimes found safety in a friend's garage, or slept in dog parks. No one cared. By fifteen, Gord was using drugs to numb the pain.

Gord was invited to leave home, but many homeless youth are fleeing abuse, neglect or other untenable family situations. Most often, the adults know something's wrong long before these children become homeless. Child welfare may get involved. Some youngsters can cycle through several foster homes and group homes before ending up on the streets. Our youth need to be managed and supported long before a street gang lures them into crime.

Gord's fondest childhood memory was a cold winter night when he was caught in the back alley of a convenience store with a loaf of bread, a box of Twinkies and a bottle of Coke. Gord joked that at least he was half full. As Gord was being carted off to the police station that night, he felt good knowing that he would be treated to a warm bed and a cold breakfast.

Gord never went back to Maplehurst. He completed his time at OCI, never missing a class, always smiling in the back row—a welcome guest. Gord would often stay behind for a chat, making my day. It was the closest I ever got to John Wayne.

By the time Gord was graduating, we had developed a solid friendship. At his final class, he thanked me for my "glorious gig" and wished me well. I gave him a motivational top-up. He was leaving the next day, so my "choose life" topic was timely.

Gord was going to stay with Aunt Maryanne. She lived in a rather seedy Toronto neighbourhood, but she was kind enough to drop off a few transportation dollars and a winter coat.

As we chatted, Gord promised that he would stay off heroin. We talked about harm reduction and how he could switch to a less potent drug. He also vowed to continue attending Narcotics Anonymous meetings and give life a try. I was elated.

Just before leaving the auditorium, Gord gave me a gift. His legacy, if you will. "Phyllis," he said lowering his voice to a whisper, "the boys said that if you thought you could help us, you'd crawl across the auditorium floor to deliver the goods."

"And I agree," he added.

So what could go wrong?

The following Monday, as I approached the auditorium, Gord's buddy Stuart stopped me in the hallway. He knew that Gord and I were friends, and he whispered that he had some very bad news.

Stuart dropped his head in respect and in a somber voice said, "Gord overdosed. He passed away this morning, Phyllis. I'm so sorry."

"I can't believe this. We just said goodbye, Stuart." I collapsed against the wall. "He promised he would lay off the heroin. What happened?"

"We have no details. One of the guards told me this morning." Stuart's sadness was apparent. No one ever learned if it was an accident or intentional suicide.

I was stunned. Moments later when I began to cry, the men gave me a chair and some privacy. A sick feeling of loss came over me. And a sense of failure. For months, I questioned where I went wrong. What more I could have said to Gord?

It is still difficult to believe that the world has lost Gord Boyd.

Examining my work with him gave me with a chance to explore my professional uncertainties and many imperfections. This is something I continue to work on. Recognizing my weaknesses and attempting to grow from that awareness is meaningful.

Accepting my personal challenges and discussing them openly gives others a platform to address their own humanity and accept that we all fail from time to time. The pain of losing Gord has invoked great humility, but I have learned to seek wisdom in everything. And that includes my failures.

Dear Gord. As we say in the Jewish tradition, "may your memory be for a blessing."

CHAPTER THIRTEEN

The mother of all healing

HOW DO WE FORGIVE someone who has deeply hurt us? Or, perhaps more dishearteningly, how do we forgive ourselves for something we have done to hurt others?

Forgiveness may be defined as a conscious and deliberate decision to release feelings of resentment or hate towards a person (or group) who has wronged us, regardless of their deservedness.

Life is so much richer when we let go of the guilt we feel for something we've done or the pent up resentment we have toward others. When we learn to forgive wholeheartedly, we are able to love and be loved more deeply.

Despite these wonderful perks, granting forgiveness is a choice. And choosing not to forgive does not make you a bad person. Experts say that forcing or faking forgiveness is counterproductive because it often leaves us with feelings of anxiety, anger or depression. If forgiveness isn't possible, another option is to unburden the past, move into the present and live your best future in order to begin the healing process.

In forgiving my father, it was helpful for me to recall not only his flaws but also his virtues. While some victims must search deep for these little gems, remembering such virtues is a wonderful and welcome aid to healing. Although I shall never fully forget Dad's dirty deeds, forgiveness has led to less vivid and visited memories.

Friends say I'm a frequent forgiver. When Lenny (my first husband) walked out after eleven years of marriage, I was able to forgive him with minimal effort. We married young. I focused my thoughts on the future. After a twenty-four-hour cry and a twelve-week diet, life was good. The degree of hurt will often determine the difficulty of letting go. Take whatever time you need, but remember that the person who hurt you has already found their way home.

Do you know someone who's angry? Of course, you do. It's easy to spot these warriors; they're always looking to do battle. Angry people have a revolving tale of woe. There's one in every grocery store lineup. They are mad at the cashier because the gummies aren't stocked, and when the cashier says, "Hi, how are you today?" these fighters lash out.

Difficult people, you know who you are. Everyone has a past, but some people have never learned forgiveness. They work at having a reputation for anger that's honed and easily triggered. But anger never serves them.

For all you grudge-holders, we know forgiveness is not always easy, but it sure is liberating. A sacred and pivotal moment will present when the burden of resentment melts into a release of anger and a feeling of freedom. Notice it and feel it because, at that moment, life will present some interesting and exhilarating possibilities.

Compassion plays a vital role when it comes to forgiveness: both granting (victim) and receiving (transgressor). In order to truly forgive, a victim must have the ability to put themselves in the transgressor's place just long enough to understand and feel a bit of compassion. This allows for forgiveness to flow more naturally.

In addition, forgiveness is more likely to occur when an emotionally intelligent transgressor is able to express sincere compassion, guilt and remorse for their wrongdoings and an emotionally intelligent victim has compassion and understanding.

Haven't we all been there?

In more critical situations, a professionally certified mediator should be called upon. As one myself, I have done considerable work in the area of forgiveness on both sides of the prison wall. Mediation can be helpful and is designed to work with two adversarial individuals or teams. (When working with teams, it's preferable to have one spokesperson represent each team to prevent any "ganging up" dynamic.) The following approach has never failed me when all parties are seriously motivated:

For Starters:
Set a convenient time and place for the "adult" conversation.

Limit the number of items to be discussed and offer only one item at a time. The grocery list approach is never helpful and may lead to nasty results.

Be open and honest but not insulting.

Listen to one another without distraction, interruption, electronic devices or kids.

Consider the other person's perspective.

Seek to understand both the facts and the feelings.

Ask clarifying questions and paraphrase back your understanding of what your adversary is saying.

The Process:
First party discusses their facts, findings and feelings until they feel understood.

Second party discusses their facts, findings and feelings until they feel understood.

Repeat steps 1 and 2, as required.

When the conversation is completed, determine and clearly state what everyone agrees upon. It will help to write it down.

Determine and clearly state what still remains unresolved. It will help to write it down.

Finally, negotiate a solution for each outstanding point. Again, write it down.

In negotiating the outstanding issues, you are aiming for a winning outcome that satisfies both sides. This will involve compromise. It's most notable that mediation is only successful when both parties are motivated to move on and feel they got a fair shake.

During the successful mediation process, both parties will have a clearer understanding about the origin of hurt. Most often, both parties will have had some responsibility in creating the hurt, even if it was just a mixed message or an unfounded assumption.

An apology is the gift of damage control. It's a tool we use to acknowledge a violation, take responsibility for an action, ask forgiveness and try to repair the relationship. An effective apology has these components:

An acknowledgment of responsibility.

A statement of empathy.

An explanation (not a defence).

A statement of regret and request for forgiveness.

An assurance of improved future behaviour (promise only what you can deliver).

The most important component of any apology is the empathy statement. In order for an injured person to truly forgive, they need to know that the offender understands the full impact of their actions. Developing empathy, and the ability to express it authentically, is the key to developing and maintaining healthy relationships.

The ability to forgive is a sign of integrity, emotional maturity and intelligence. It is one of the great virtues to which we should all aspire. "Forgiveness is not an occasional act; it is a constant attitude," said Martin Luther King Jr.

Every inmate that I encountered wished desperately that they could turn back time. Ah, the universal do-over of a second chance. Although time is irreversible, the future presents a world of choices.

CHAPTER FOURTEEN

Rape, regret and remorse

THESE DAYS, I BEGIN my forgiveness lesson with the devastating story of Josh, a serial rapist. He had handed me a carefully folded note after class one day, asking how he could even think of forgiving himself for his horrific sins:

How does one forgive himself of his wrongdoings when he knows his victims never would, especially when there could be as many as . . . lots of them.

Done this harm for a quarter of his life. Due to his actions he has severely harmed a large number of victims, possibly costing them their lives?

Cannot get, or would never get . . . their forgiveness.

And the loved ones of these victims have been hurt too, after finding out what he has done to their family. For these victims to truly forgive him, to even ask for forgiveness is out of the question.

No chance to ever consider forgiving himself because he believes he does not deserve it. What should he do?

· Josh

After reading Josh's note, I was shaken, sad and bordering on queasy. Disturbed by my own reaction, I questioned my ability to make a positive impact. Ultimately, rape is not an easy thing to face or to forgive.

Not all rapists are created equally. Experts classify sexual attackers into four main categories:

The Polite Rapist: He is driven to compulsive behaviour by deep feelings of general inadequacy—not necessarily sexual inadequacy. Often, he is shy, a loner, an underachiever and may feel dominated by his regular partner. This rapist is polite and tries to involve his victim, exhibiting signs of affection by kissing and stuff. He fantasizes that the sex is consensual and the victim is enjoying it. Some perpetrators even ask their victim to compare their sexual performance to that of others or request a "second date."

The Entitled Rapist: He operates on the assumption that women owe him something—and that something is sex. Masking his doubts with strong and aggressive masculine behaviour, this offender only feels like a man once he seizes whatever he came to get.

The Raging Rapist: He is angry at the world and, often, at a particular woman or women in general. A wrong or a perceived wrong ignites an attack, usually within hours. He acts on impulse, often using debilitating force. Once his rage is spent, he is unlikely to rape again until stresses crescendo into a full-scale eruption.

The Ritual Rapist: He is a brutal rapist, void of empathy and possessing deep psychopathic traits. This profile accounts for only 10 per cent of sexual assaults, yet often makes the headlines. This rapist uses ritualism— bondage or sadism. His victims are vulnerable women whom he can easily control. Aroused by his victim's suffering, their pain and discomfort will encourage him, particularly if they struggle to escape. This torture often culminates in murder.

Josh was a small, awkward, unfortunate-looking man. With a strange comb-over that fell onto his face and thick round glasses, it was difficult to see his eyes. He appeared damaged and was severely introverted. Josh never had visitors, so it was unlikely that he had any external support or felt loved.

Josh had spent months in the third row, second seat from the end, disappearing into the crowd and never saying a word. He never smiled. Come to think of it, he never showed any emotion. I know the look. It's the look of someone who is severely damaged, in deep emotional pain and feeling shamed. It's a dangerous mix.

I had a week to think about my response to Josh's note. I knew this was a valuable teaching opportunity. If I handled Josh with care, perhaps we would both have a breakthrough moment.

Desperately uncertain but searching for wisdom to encourage healing for Josh, I began to obsess on Google. I searched "forgiveness when my sins are overwhelming."

After hours spent seeking guidance on the internet, I needed a stiff shrink. The web usually has an answer. It didn't. I tried to find it from within. I couldn't. And of course I was becoming more uncertain with each moment, doubting myself, questioning if I could provide Josh a gateway to healing. "The whole problem with the world is that fools and fanatics are always so certain of themselves, and wiser people so full of doubts," said Bertrand Russell.

After the fruitless search, I went to lunch with Frances, a friend from the neighbourhood. Frances, an attractive and petite woman, is a sixty-year-old golf and tennis self-declared master. By her own admission, Frances has a smaller heart than most, but her intelligence and humour had earned my respect. We had been friends for eons. I thought I knew her.

While struggling for a revelation to help Josh, divine intervention was coming. Just how hands-on is God? And what if he actually does intervene—leaving no footprint behind—in world affairs?

Frances and I were enjoying gossip and giggles over cake and quiche. Gossip is not an ethical formula for a ladies' lunch, is it? But this coincidence is sound evidence that the universe cares about everyone—or perhaps everyone who chooses to forsake bad for good.

My revelation came as we were chatting about Marla, who was having an emotional affair with her disinterested boss. Nonchalantly, Frances let slip that she had enjoyed an electrifying extramarital affair five years earlier. An affair. As in real sex and lots of it.

"Frances, oh my God! You?" I squealed. I was shocked that Frances had closed the deal and failed to reveal. I mean, an eternity of sinful sandwiches and this went untold?

"It was a midlife crisis," she said, making it sound like a car accident. "I mean, it hit me while I was walking the dog."

With a proud smile of accomplishment, she threw her head back as if she had deserved a matrimonial break, or at least a break from monogamy. And I was thinking: Try not to judge her.

Damn it, she had upstaged me just as I was about to announce the end of my own monotonous marriage.

Frances and Morris had been married for twenty years. Second marriage for both. Morris was not only pleasing to the eye, he was intelligent and actually quite wonderful. You know, the kind of guy you wish you had married. Frances, still happily married to Morris at sixty, had been suffering a mid-fifties crisis.

"Frances, are you telling me you had an affair while you were married to Morris?"

"A fantastic year," was her prideful declaration with narrowed eyes and a raised shoulder that questioned my shock. She went on to promote the merits of hot sex with a cool stranger and how to manage the inevitable homecoming to a loving and over-sexed husband.

Look at that! Frances was a polished adulteress. And she made extra sex sound marvellous, especially given my own current drought. Pleased that the universe might hand out some badass inspiration that day, I pressed on.

"Did you feel guilty, Frances?

"This is what you ask?" she said curiously.

"Yes. Actually, I'm working with a rapist," I declared, anxious to examine a guilty mind.

"Well, I don't feel guilt anymore. But at first, sure, kind of."

Okay, maybe she has a deeply imbedded moral compass, but clearly it's not visible. Nor is it perfect—splendid!

"I need to understand something on a deeper level, Frances. It has to do with my guys." Hoping she understood that 'my guys' referred to a prison audience.

"Yes?" she asked, looking perplexed as in, what don't you get?

"When the affair ended, you stayed with Morris. Business as usual, right? How were things for you? I mean, were you able to forgive yourself?" I probed, leaning into the table as the waiter dropped off more cream.

I paused for the waiter to leave and then asked gently, not wanting to embarrass her, "Could you forgive yourself? I mean, could you move on with those feelings of guilt?"

Frances responded slowly, looking skyward as if she were reliving a blessed event, "When the affair with Brad ended, I felt horrible about what I had done to Morris."

My God, she does have a compass. "Yes, go on," I whispered from the edge of my chair.

"So, in moving beyond what I had done, I vowed that I would never again jeopardize our marriage. I went out of my way to be kinder, more considerate, more loving. Every. Single. Day." She said this slowly and with the emphasis on "every."

There it was. My inspiration.

When dealing with sex offenders, it's difficult for me to get beyond their horrific deeds and give them my heart. But no prisoner is mine to judge. Learning the background of a sex offender has helped my counselling. And, although it doesn't excuse them, it's useful to understand the trauma that underlies their behaviour. I find that partnering with prisoners begins with connection. And connection can only be achieved when you feel a reasonable measure of compassion.

To that point, Josh was not born to privilege. Like many sex offenders, Josh was a sexual assault victim himself. He survived extreme violence and repeated sexual abuse, involving multiple family members, at home. Including Mom.

Childhood sexual abuse leaves the victim feeling fear, shame, humiliation, guilt and even self-blame. These emotions can lead to depression and anxiety. Survivors often develop a belief that they caused the sexual abuse or that they deserved it, resulting in self-destructive relationships or worse.

When I returned to prison the following week, I felt empowered and anxious to speak with Josh after class.

"Josh, I read your note. It created a full spectrum of emotion in me. I felt anger, and I felt sadness. I was confused and I feared that I wouldn't have a response for you, one that might begin the healing process. And that upset me too."

"I'm sorry," he mouthed.

"But here's the thing, Josh. I'm proud of you for taking responsibility for your actions. I'm proud of you for sharing your heart with me. And I'm proud of you for understanding how serious your offences are."

"Yes, you severely scarred and traumatized each of your victims in a perverse, painful and damaging way. That was wrong and that was selfish. As you said in your note, Josh, because of your behaviour they will suffer for the rest of their lives. Is that right?"

I needed an acknowledgement and a show of remorse. It was painful for me to speak like that to Josh—a person who was so deeply wounded. I would have preferred to comfort him. But I knew the approach I was taking might benefit him more.

"Yes," he responded firmly. Though clearly shaken, he was also engaged.

"We can agree that you can't go back and undo any of the tragedy and trauma that you've caused," I declared, reinforcing the egregious nature of his past acts of violence.

Josh sat silently across from me, made eye contact and blinked. I saw his pain and felt his shame. We were both uncomfortable.

"So, here's what we're going to do, Josh."

Josh sat motionless but then offered a half-nod.

"First, continue to focus on your thoughts and emotions and then on your healthy goals and ambitions. It's crucial that you concentrate on areas that need development. And follow the advice of our professionals here by taking notes and reviewing them often. There's much work to do Josh, but you can do this!"

"Yes," he said loudly, as if he felt hopeful. Ah, a clue that this was time well spent.

"And Josh, although it's painful and very difficult, I would like you to find some forgiveness for the abuse you suffered. If you can find some compassion, Josh . . ."

"I will try," he said in an agonized whisper. "I want to be a better person. I can be a better person, Phyllis."

The shift was undeniable and delivered with a trace of enthusiasm. I smiled at Josh to acknowledge my assent and then paused.

"Now the next part will shock you, Josh," I continued. "You must also work on forgiving yourself. It's tough, the toughest part, perhaps. It seems impossible and undeserving, doesn't it? But, in order for you to move beyond the shame, the shame that's holding you back from healing, you must first forgive yourself."

"How?" he asked.

"Okay, my advice will help you move on, Josh. I ask that you spend the rest of your life bestowing kindness on everyone. It could be a simple smile. Or listening to a friend, helping a friend, being there for others, even strangers. At first, it may be awkward. Josh, it's critical to forgive in order to move away from the pain and devastation of your past. If you don't practice forgiveness, there's a much greater risk of reoffending. We don't want that."

"Phyllis, I've been to every class at OCI. I've attended your program. I've attended the Sexual Offending Relapse Prevention Program. I want this. I gave you that note because I think it's my last chance for a real change."

I began to feel encouraged.

"Josh, the concept is simple, but it's not easy. This is the hardest part of your journey. I understand that you want this, and I think you're ready. You must begin to move away from the pain and hurt that has harmed you. And you must move away from the pain and hurt that you've caused. I need you to promise me and promise yourself, that your life is about kindness now. Because it works. From this moment on, you will live the best version of yourself, Josh. Every. Single. Day."

He nodded in agreement. His remorse was so intense, he began sobbing uncontrollably. In that moment, I felt the release of his pain and the possibility of a breakthrough. And I cried too.

Hugging an inmate is strictly forbidden, but I stood up and gave Josh a big fat emotional hug. Screw the risk! I'm firmly focused on the reward.

"Remember, Josh, layers and layers of kindness."

After that, Josh attended every class until his release date. For almost two years, he was attentive, made copious notes and occasionally stayed behind to chat. All good.

Josh was making a gallant effort to learn about himself and heal. When the day came for Josh to leave OCI, we talked at length about what life would be like on the outside. My preparedness talk has earned a reputation for being cogent. Josh was going to live in a halfway home that transitions previously incarcerated men into society. A stellar opportunity for continued therapy.

Did I heal Josh? Heck no, I wasn't born with healing powers or angel mist. But Josh, highly motivated and working with professionals, has an opportunity for change. I pray that he dedicates the rest of his life to kindness. And it's comforting to think that he will.

CHAPTER FIFTEEN

A tale of two pretties

WHILE I WORKED AT the law firm, I took courses in teaching, training and counselling. In the years after I was fired, I took more courses to become a certified life coach and mediator. I gathered a broad base of people who felt they needed a boost.

Beyond the prison walls, friends would approach me for guidance and often refer another for counselling. Two of my clients were an interesting, long-established couple. These ladies had enjoyed an adoring and meaningful relationship, which had grown increasingly special over twenty years.

They began as roommates. Shirley had been previously married, but Laverne had not, and neither had children. Shirley was known as Dior for her sparkles and girliness. Laverne, more masculine and sporty, was referred to as John Deere.

Their initial goal was to pool their financial resources and buy a comfortable home, just to get into the real estate game. But the game evolved into love. They liked the same entertainment, created a circle of friends, lived to dine, loved to travel and, above all, loved one another dearly. A marvellous enough life.

Not completely. Over the years, Laverne had exhibited some very offensive and inappropriate anger, often directing it at Shirley. These anger episodes grew worse with time and were lasting longer, so fortunately they sought help. And that's when I entered the picture.

During our sessions, I learned that Laverne had lived through some tough experiences that resulted from her father's behaviour. Her dad was an unforgiving, non-forgetting Holocaust survivor, and Laverne's childhood difficulties fed her anger.

Regardless of the origin story, excessive anger cannot be tolerated. While we all experience anger occasionally, getting stuck in an anger cycle is damaging. Anger erodes trust, breaks down communication and blasts through love. In fact, there is no quicker way to make your partner feel isolated and alone than to exhibit anger, especially violent anger.

After several years of carefully managing this anger, Shirley became distressed over Laverne's relentless provocations. Finally, she packed her bags and without a word to anyone, left home. Originally from Glasgow, Shirley had lived in Toronto for forty years, but when she and Laverne fought, Glasgow offered an escape. Shirley went home for a visit with no definite plans to return.

In Scotland, she was met with a welcome that reminded her that she had options: a return to family; unconditional love; unwavering support and the kind of validation that fortifies hope.

Though I am not advocating a departure from home, this scenario gave the couple a break from the stresses of life, time to reflect and an opportunity to miss one another. And it was Christmas time. Naturally, the holiday season heightens loneliness. It became achingly clear to Laverne and Shirley that their union was about to implode.

Although painful, missing one another was good. Pain can promote an awakening. It is much easier to motivate fighters once they realize that humans move either toward pleasure or away from pain. The choice becomes simple, but the effort requires discipline.

Before long Shirley returned to Toronto and reunited with Laverne, but the couple remained very unsure of their future and trust was eroding. In order to survive, trust needs a chance to build and show consistency.

Establishing that the ladies both desperately wanted to save their relationship, I asked them to invoke the forgiveness clause. It was critical that they begin to heal the relationship by letting the past go. A new beginning meant leaving anger behind and building trust. A pivot, where both their words and actions came from kindness.

I gave the ladies a copy of my Anger Management booklet and the same mantra that I gave Josh, the serial rapist. "Layers and layers of kindness." In this case, kindness toward one another.

"If you slip up—and you will slip up," I told them, "stop the behaviour immediately and acknowledge that you need a do-over. And then invoke our kindness mantra."

They were encouraged by this instruction but still shaky.

"I assure you it works if you work it. Otherwise, kiss each other goodbye."

"In the Jewish religion, twenty-five hours a year are focused on forgiveness," I reminded them.

Yom Kippur, also known as the Day of Atonement, is considered the most sacred holiday in the Jewish faith. According to tradition, on Yom Kippur our Creator decides each person's fate. So we are encouraged to make amends and seek forgiveness for sins committed during the previous year.

My dad had his own spin on repentance. Thankfully, God is far more lenient and forgiving.

I cautioned Shirley and Laverne that there would always be clashes but, if they chose their battles and battlegrounds, they could get through any challenge. Picking the most conducive time and place to talk can help to get past a hiccup or calm a storm.

I left them to it. Two years later I had an opportunity to catch up with the ladies.

"Whenever we find ourselves overheating," Laverne said, smiling and rolling her eyes as if to add, thank God, "we remember your words: 'Layers and layers of kindness.'"

"Phyllis," she said with conviction, "it stops a lot of arguments."

Kindness is the key to life. It gives us the chance to play with others in a way that deepens friendship and gives birth to love. Continued kindness builds trust. It elects comfort over chaos.

Practice layers of kindness in your relationships and then sit back and enjoy the ride.

CHAPTER SIXTEEN

Harry and Kally

Y OU KNOW HOW WE talk about trying to see the good in everyone? How kindness and forgiveness are essential to leading a happy life? I believed that too. Until I met Harry.

Harry was an elderly man, nearing eighty. With an unsightly stomach bulging from beneath his orange sweatshirt, wispy white hair and a toothy yellow grin, Harry was simply gross.

In contrast to his appearance, however, Harry was a smart, successful businessman who boasted he had a great deal of money. Harry wanted to stand out from others. And that he did.

Harry, better educated than most prisoners, claimed two business degrees and several other academic achievements. He spoke to everyone as if they owed him something. Humility would have been more attractive, but boasting was Harry's thing. It was obvious to me that Harry's fuel tank was low on sensitivity and high on narcissism.

Harry's incessant boasting and arrogance made him unpopular with inmates and even less popular with the guards. I ignored him. In fact, I didn't want to work with Harry. Nevertheless, the life of a volunteer . . .

One gloomy Monday afternoon following my Forgiveness lesson, Harry and I were the only two left in the auditorium. He pulled up a chair beside me and announced that we were going to chat. His aura of entitlement was off-putting, but I respectfully agreed.

Harry told me he had a son, Kenneth, who had married late in life but now had a loving wife and a pretty ten-year-old daughter, Kally.

"Harry, what would you like to discuss today?"

"Well, I've been sitting here thinking about this forgiveness thing," Harry began. "I'd sure as hell like a bit of forgiveness from my family," he announced in a resentful and angry tone that suggested they should know better.

"Sure, Harry. Very often there is a path to forgiveness, particularly when genuine remorse is expressed," I said, restating the lesson.

"Damn. I'm angry with my entire family right now," he spewed. "It's just not fair! My family's trying to send me away. They're asking me to give up my home. Actually, they're asking me to move away. Far away."

Harry said that he had lived in the same small rural town all his life and bragged of having "the home he deserved," a magnificent house.

"I see, Harry. Why do they want you to move?"

"It's because of my charges."

Notice that he used the word "charges," not crimes. Harry is a convicted pedophile.

"They say I'm no longer a part of the family. They want me out. My own son wished me dead," he said with venom and a deep scowl.

"That's sad, Harry. Do you have any idea why they might feel that way?" I asked, dreading what might come next.

Harry sat thinking for a moment or two, as if trying to find the right words, or at least something that would win me over. "It started with my wife," he continued. "Years ago. She began to ignore me. I mean we were just moving further and further apart until there was nothing. It wasn't a marriage."

"Harry, were you living with your wife before coming to OCI?"

"Yes. Don't think she'll have me back though. She never visits."

"Is there more, Harry?"

"A few years ago, when my wife and I were growing apart, I started feeling lonely. Alone.

Unwanted."

I'm thinking: I'll bet.

"Actually, no one was really interested in me." He sighed. "No one except for my granddaughter,

Kally. Kally and I were . . . We often . . . we met in the basement. I mean for movies. Kally liked to watch that Frozen movie."

"Kally always cuddled up with me when we watched movies. We loved cuddling. It felt good, really good having someone close. Kally would sort of show affection, you know," he said, flashing a joyous smile.

I needed a pause just to breathe through what was coming. "How old is Kally again?" I asked.

"She was ten when we started watching movies. Such beautiful long black hair."

"Go on, Harry."

"After several months of watching movies, I began to touch Kally. You know, just touch."

I'm thinking: I don't need details.

In retrospect, I should have summarized the problem and stopped the conversation. Harry was reliving his joy as he described what came next.

"Kally never stopped me," he continued. "I kind of thought maybe she liked it. I guess I was telling myself she liked it. And then it just seemed to progress . . . it . . . well . . . it morphed."

I kept my face blank to appear emotionless, but my breath was shallow and my heart was pounding.

Harry concluded, "One evening when we were alone, I penetrated Kally. I wasn't thinking straight that night. It just happened. It all happened so quickly. Kally was quiet the whole time. Not crying. Nothing. And then I . . ."

"Stop Harry, I understand now."

I'm thinking: You bastard. You are such a fucking bastard.

"But when we finished, Kally ran upstairs screaming, screaming so the entire family could hear." He was actually blaming the young girl.

And notice that he said, "when we finished." In his sick mind, Kally had partnered with him—until she didn't.

"So here I am," he said, raising both hands, palms up. And he looked me straight in the eye, pausing for my reaction.

Harry had no remorse. No shame. I had just heard a repugnant account of child rape: Pedophilia by Granddad. By the time this incident took place, my daughter Melanie was married, and I had recently become a Gramma. I was intensely repulsed. I had no idea what to say or do.

My initial reaction was to stand up and walk out. Or to explain that I couldn't respond, couldn't continue, couldn't counsel. My brain was screaming to get out of the room. Instead, I paused my breathing and stopped blinking. My heart hurt. I was revolted and filled with loathing, but I took a moment.

I composed myself for the sake of Harry's family.

"Harry, what is your family asking of you?"

"They're asking me to move out of town. I'm really angry," he bellowed, as if he was entitled to something better. "I wanted to speak with you because I don't want to move. It's ridiculous. I'm an old man now. My entire life is in Centreville."

"How does my family expect me to pick up and move? At my age? My wife's leaving me. My son's not speaking with me. I'll have no one."

He looked at me pleadingly, as if I could change that. And I'm thinking: Good for them. You should've thought of that before you hurt that little girl.

I'm not sure where I got the courage, but in the calmest tone I said, "Harry, what you've done to your family is a sin. There is no do-over. No forgiveness. Nothing. In short, it's the ultimate betrayal. An act that is inhumane."

There are too many Kallys in the world. Murder, torture and abuse, particularly of a child, is unforgivable and incomprehensible.

"Kally is deeply scarred for life, Harry. Your family is asking you to move away. That's the least you can do for them. The least you can do to allow them to begin the healing process."

"I have no idea what your future holds, Harry, or if there could ever be a path to forgiveness. But, at the very least, you owe them this."

"Phyllis," he said slowly, "every case worker, psychologist, even the inmates, said the same thing. But they said it differently. I wanted to ask you because they say you're fair. Compassionate."

Trust me, I had no compassion for Harry.

"I promised myself I would listen to you." Harry looked sad. He looked sad because this outcome would affect him.

I was praying that Harry wouldn't say another word. I wanted him to go and leave me alone. Taking his time, he stood up and, without another word, sauntered out.

Recalling this story brings back ugly memories that make me physically ill. Harry's granddaughter is scarred for life. She will be traumatized and require intense counselling.

Sadly, these children often wind up with severe emotional illness or in deep psychological pain that ends in substance abuse or addictive behaviour (sex, gambling, self-injury).

A malignant outcome because of one man's reckless behaviour.

I see my role in the prison system as twofold. First, to provide guidance and second, hope. But being disingenuous is not part of the job. Generally, I use my influence to be of service to the prisoners. This time, I was not rooting for the prisoner.

But perhaps I was of service to his family.

CHAPTER SEVENTEEN

Gratitude: Alex and Sandy

H OW WOULD LIFE BE if you were totally satisfied with what you have? No need to wish upon a star; your constellation already spells gratitude.

I'm not suggesting that we shouldn't strive to set goals and do better. But we should pause to appreciate that our glass is—already—rather full.

Gratitude has strong transformative powers. If you're experiencing sadness, anxiety or depression during a crisis, gratitude is a psychological defence that unleashes the power of now.

Did your mother ever tell you, "No one has everything?"

Gratitude is the grown-up word for thankfulness. Some say it's a discipline rather than a feeling, and it begins by noticing quiet pleasures. It means living life as if everything is a miracle and being aware of our blessings. It means looking at what we have and not comparing it with what they have.

Our brains cannot be in a state of appreciation and a state of fear at the same time. So, experiencing gratitude can be helpful to those who feel down or overwhelmed.

Appreciating all we have and receive, whether tangible or intangible is the antithesis of expectation. Let's pause to acknowledge the goodness in our lives because it connects us with something larger than ourselves – whether to souls, nature or a higher power.

We're not born with gratitude. It's a conscious choice we make to live life in appreciation. Behavioural and psychological research has shown gratitude can lead to unexpected life improvements. At the Ontario Correctional Centre, where inmates face profound daily challenges, feeling grateful is a big deal.

When I give my Gratitude lesson in the prison system, I begin by asking inmates for their examples. It's fascinating how enthusiastic they are to share. Their comments are moving, illuminating and extremely humbling. The prisoners are educating me on the impact of gratefulness.

"I got a letter from my girlfriend today," James says, acknowledging that a letter is a gift.

"My family is still supporting me after everything," Kent beams with pride and appreciation.

"I've got a heated room and a roof over my head," Todd says, referring to his jail cell in the dead of winter.

"I just had a hot lunch today," Richard shares, as if a meal is a miracle.

"OCI has very few brawls," Tom announces, grateful for the culture of a treatment-centric prison.

"I'm six months clean and sober," Kevin declares as the room becomes electric.

"Motivational Mondays!" Andrew exclaims and the applause begins.

Focusing on gratitude has a deep impact on our well-being. Studies show that keeping a daily journal of gratitude boosts alertness, enthusiasm, determination, optimism and energy. All of that increases our dopamine, the feel-good neurotransmitter, which encourages greater productivity and lessens depression.

As a result, those who practice gratitude tend to be more creative, recover more quickly from adversity (resiliency), have stronger immune systems and have more meaningful relationships.

At OCI, inmates are required to keep a gratitude journal. This journal is not necessarily private and can be reviewed by officials at any time, but many of my guys report that it has lifted them up, even on their darkest days.

To say we feel grateful is not to say that everything in our lives is great. It just means that we're aware of the goodness and abundance that surrounds us rather than taking it for granted.

Speaking of gratitude, a decade ago I bumped into a public schoolmate while attending a shiva. Carolyn recognizing me was a pure delight. Within weeks, we organized a reunion and, being a compatible group, began meeting every few months.

When COVID-19 locked us down, the "Glen Rush Girls" began regular Zoom meetups and took turns sharing our silver linings. Indeed, lock down had an upside; we were bonding à la pandemic. Supporting and loving each other in a time of intense uncertainty was a bonding uplift and we are very grateful. Right, girls?

When you focus on the positive aspects of your life, you will begin to see changes. If you want to attract positivity, show gratitude, appreciation and love for the people and things around you. As your thoughts and language become more positive, you will begin to attract positive people and situations into your life. "Acknowledging the good that you already have in your life is the foundation for all abundance," says Eckhart Tolle.

During one of my sessions on Gratitude, I asked if anyone would like to share a story. In an auditorium of avid learners, a fellow at the back began vigorously waving his hand, obviously eager to catch my attention.

"And what's your name," I asked, matching his enthusiasm.

"Alex."

"Yes, Alex, what are you grateful for today?"

"I'm grateful for Saturday morning phone calls," he said, with a deep expansive smile.

"Wonderful, Alex. Did you have a nice phone call this weekend?"

"Yes! But this is about my call six months ago."

Joy was spreading through a sea of smiling faces. The inmates knew what was coming.

"Interesting, Alex. What was this call about?"

"Well, six months ago, I called the wrong number, and Alice answered the phone."

"Who's Alice?"

"Well, Alice was a wrong number."

He had my attention.

"We can only call collect from here, you know. And the person we're calling has to accept the call and pay the charges. Alice accepted my call."

"Oh. My. Gosh," I said, eagerly waiting on more.

The men knew the Alice story, and everyone was watching my expression. Have I told you I'm often quite animated? The guys seemed more interested in my reaction than the actual story.

"Well, Alice and I spoke for a full twenty minutes. We talked about so many things. Like a first date, kind of. And then she asked if maybe I'd call her again."

For inmates in Ontario's correctional institutions, connecting with family, friends and lawyers is a challenge. Their calls are limited to twenty minutes and even local calling charges rack up quickly. And these days, everyone on the outside has a cellphone, but inmates can't make a collect call to a mobile phone (although this may be changing).

Now I was smiling and feeling a bit emotional. Alex continued.

"So, I called Alice the next Saturday, and then the next Saturday, and then every Saturday."

I was thrilled and everyone was smiling. Best prison story ever.

Giving Alex's story the attention it deserved, I ask the audience, "Is this really happening, guys? Wow, how special is all this!"

Beaming now, Alex nodded with a pride that was dreamlike. He was feeling a sense of belonging for the first time in his life and his happiness was unmistakable. And contagious.

"After a few months of talking every Saturday," he continued, "Alice came to visit me. She came here. And now she comes here every week."

Alex had touched my heart.

"Alice, she's waiting for me to get out. I'm done in five months and we're planning a future. A wedding. Kids."

Alex was thirty-three.

For a bit of background, at three months of age, Alex was left on a church doorstep. He was then tossed from foster home to foster home until he reached the age of majority. He never felt loved by anyone and was never able to connect with people in what we would consider healthy relationships.

Before OCI, Alex was a career drug dealer with no possibility of a healthy future and little chance of pulling himself out a dangerous criminal life. But that accidental Saturday morning phone call to Alice upended his universe.

Alex told Alice that he lived in a prison, but she had heard gated community. It's all in the point of view.

After class, Alex shared a bit more with me privately. It seems that before Alex's call that day, Alice had been feeling lonely and quite isolated. After suffering a life of bullying and racial prejudice, Alice had given up on people. But, when she described herself to Alex that Saturday morning, all he said was, "Can't wait to meet cha."

Since his release, Alex has stayed out of trouble. Indeed, he and Alice are still a thing.

Studies show that when an ex-con has a strong connection on the outside, they have a decent chance of succeeding. Alex's connection to Alice gives him a better second chance at life. And maybe a baby of his own one day.

Lady Luck, you done good.

Here's another gratitude story; this one from my class in the women's prison.

Sandy was a fairly attractive slim brunette and very popular. She had a refreshing air of professionalism. Sandy had been a respected oncology nurse with a great career. Like many of us, Sandy had worked hard to be excellent at her job. She had devoted her life to her passion.

Following a complicated hysterectomy, Sandy was prescribed pain killers. When they ran out, Sandy helped herself to the hospital supply upon returning to work. It's a common story. And a tragic one for Sandy— she may never return to nursing. At times, Sandy exhibited warning signs of hopelessness.

One day Sandy came to class and announced that she was having thoughts about suicide. That day, I worked with Sandy until her survival motivator kicked in. Following class, however, I was obligated to report the incident to prison professionals. I prayed for her recovery and the next week, Sandy thanked me for saving her life. In that moment, I realized the true meaning of giving back.

Today, in Gratitude class, Sandy wanted to share.

"I'd like to go first," Sandy said. "I've been thinking about this all week."

"Sandy, we would love to hear from you," I said, happy for a hint of enthusiasm.

"Well, I'm very excited. I was just moved to Unit 3."

"Sandy, were you not getting along on your unit?" I asked curiously.

"I'm not really sure why they switched me out, but I'm genuinely pleased," she said.

"Well, either way Sandy, I'm happy for you."

That was it, I thought, and I went on to ask the next attendee what they were grateful for, but before anyone could answer, Sandy leapt from her chair and was standing.

"I wasn't quite finished, Phyllis," she announced excitedly.

Everyone looked at Sandy, and the room fell unusually silent. My goodness, it's never quiet in a women's prison.

"In my new cell," Sandy continued, "I have a window. Sort of."

"How wonderful, Sandy, that is very special. Has it been comforting to look out of the window?"

"Well, it's not actually a window," she continued. "More of a small crack in the cement."

"What can you see?"

"I discovered that if I crank my head the right way, I can see daylight. And, for me, daylight's a sign of hope."

She was beaming like a kid at a fireworks display.

That afternoon, I recognized that people experience gratitude relative to their situation. For Sandy, gratitude came as a glimmer of light that acted like a beacon of hope.

Sandy would leave prison in a few months but in the meantime, a little crack in the cement gave her peace, helping her transcend from confinement to comfort.

Do you think that the privileged among us would appreciate cranking their necks for a ray of light? What does this say about us? And what does it say about gratitude?

It occurs to me that those who have the least, appreciate the most. It's often said that gratitude changes everything.

CHAPTER EIGHTEEN

Love shouldn't hurt

ROMANTIC RELATIONSHIPS HAVE brought people love, joy and cozy connection dating back to Adam and Eve. They have also caused great heartache and unbearable pain. Still, most of us either have a romantic relationship or want one. And we all love to talk about them.

I've heard many a lively tale over lunch with the ladies. At couples' gatherings, relationship talk is a definite crowd pleaser and often the subject of great humour, both dirty and clean.

In the prison system, we examine intimate relationships closely to help make critical, life-altering, decisions about new beginnings.

In providing relationship guidance, I find it fascinating how some people choose to hang in, even in the face of serious adversity (abuse, addiction, violence), while others cut and run over a basic misdemeanour.

Here's what I know for sure.

We can't necessarily understand the choices that others make, but, being human, we have opinions. We must remember that each person is unique, each relationship is unique and everyone's circumstances are different. You can have an opinion, but there is no reason to criticize someone for staying in a relationship and even less reason to criticize them for getting out.

Years ago, the late Dr. Henry Fenigstein, a Holocaust survivor and well-known psychiatrist, told me that there's an important distinction between a judgment and an opinion. I have never forgotten his teachings and apply them when encouraging others.

An opinion is what we believe to be true, but with the awareness that we may not have all the facts and are therefore open to change. Social influence (including media) is the process by which we adapt our opinions, revise beliefs, or change behaviour as a result of our interactions with others. These external influences form our personal philosophies and concepts of right and wrong.

A judgment is believing our truth is the only truth and leaves no room for the viewpoint of others. Without knowing all the facts, we leave no wiggle room for a change of mind or, for that matter, a change of heart. A judgment is labelling that encourages hate and promotes vitriol.

My romantic guidance is borne out of academic studies, confidential counselling, my personal experiences and a decade of research. To reinforce inmates who want to reform, I quote the wisdom of the great Maya Angelou:

Do the best you can until you know better.
Then, when you know better, do better.

I tell inmates that a kind of shiny red car awaits them for the roller-coaster ride outside the prison gates, but they must have the courage to drive it. I explain that courage is not the absence of fear, but the will to conquer it. As each vulnerable and frightened person takes the wheel, it's up to them how and where they drive, and who rides along.

The romantic partner who is genuinely prepared to support an ex-con has earned a place in the passenger seat, but there are other important seats too. These places must remain empty unless careful consideration is given to who is dependable, trustworthy and supportive. One wrong friend could be fatal.

Prisoners often ask if revisiting a romantic relationship is encouraged. Each case must be considered on its own merit. Telling a gang member to make new friends is easy. But asking a man to forsake his dearly loved wife of twenty years, with whom he has children, is a very different deal. One that requires careful thought.

Nevertheless, we're talking about saving lives. And so, a return to a heroin-addicted spouse or a drug-dealing parent is never okay. It is critical that if one is fragile, confused, depressed or in the process of healing, they have either a "safe spouse" or effectively no spouse at all.

I remember Dave, a young inmate, pleading with me for a return to his struggling wife, Diane (a cocaine addict and drug dealer). If he didn't go back to her, Dave told me, she would die. Thankfully, no children were involved.

In convincing Dave that he wasn't strong enough to return home, we considered the possibility of supporting Diane from afar, at least for the foreseeable future and until she cleaned up. It's painful for me to tell a loving husband not to return to his wife, but it is fundamental to his success.

In every relationship, there must be boundaries. Most of us are pretty good at distancing ourselves from toxic friends, but we have greater difficulty distancing from family, even when they are a danger to our wellbeing.

As my brother Allan said to me when I was leaving one of my marriages, "Phyllis, it's all about choices."

What follows is Trish's story—a story of violence and abuse.

I was delivering my Modern Relationships lesson to a small group of Vanier women when Trish leaned into the conversation and loudly declared, "Love shouldn't hurt."

Trish was a captivating, well-educated, mature woman in her early thirties. Unusually soft-spoken, Trish had recently become even more reserved than usual. Trish always seemed to enjoy our programming, but several months earlier she stopped attending our regular classes and we weren't able to coax her back. As other women were making friends and engaged in learning, Trish was retreating inward. Today was different though, Trish had something on her mind.

I found Trish humble and caring but sadly lacking in self-esteem. Once a government clerk, she was in prison for domestic abuse. Trish had attacked her husband in an overheated retaliation against verbal abuse and fear of physical harm. That day, her husband had not laid his hands on her, but he had before and his abuse was escalating. Trish was fighting back.

Still, on this day, Trish was the physical aggressor. And if the police believe that there are reasonable grounds that someone has committed a crime, they must charge the person. They may charge you, your partner, or both. When police are summoned, there is always a risk that you will be charged even if you are a victim.

"I want to discuss my marriage," Trish announced, appearing shaken.

"Sure, Trish, would you like time today?" I asked gently.

"Yes. I don't have a healthy relationship. I will be leaving here soon and going right back into his trap. My husband is abusive. He's mad at me all the time. Screaming mostly but physical stuff too. It's bad, really bad. And it's getting worse."

"When he screams, he makes me feel stupid, like I'm nobody. Just before coming here, it was happening every day, twice maybe. And the worst part is, I don't even know how I'm provoking him."

"Trish, I'm so sorry to hear that your situation at home is so tough. No one deserves abuse. And it's likely not even you that's provoking him. Perhaps his job, a past trauma, stress, finances. It's endless and it's common."

Trish lowered her head, and I sensed real fear from her. With a criminal record, things would be worse; she would not be able to return to her position at the government so the family would experience financial problems. With ongoing abuse, hardship and heartache awaited her.

"Trish, what are your plans when you leave Vanier?" I asked, dreading the homecoming from hell.

"I need to stay with Carl."

Her statement was gripping. It was a whisper of shame.

This was urgent. I asked the group if we could focus on Trish. The ladies nodded and appeared anxious to have this conversation.

"Trish, to be clear, are you saying that Carl is abusing you physically?"

"Yes. Yes, he's abusive. Physically, verbally and emotionally."

"Is he abusing the kids?" I probed in my gentle counselling voice, reserved for special occasions. Trish had a five-year-old daughter and a nine-month-old son.

"Not so much, mostly spanking. But he's spanking Valerie when she's done nothing. And I saw him spank the baby once, just for crying."

"Trish, we've talked about making healthy choices, but some decisions are really tough, aren't they? Leaving a husband, even an abusive one, is difficult. And it hurts like hell, even if he is dangerous. We don't want to hurt the father of our babies, and we don't want to feel as though we have somehow failed."

"Trish, leaving a man who's abusing you and is a danger to your children is not a sign of failure. It's a sign of great strength and enormous courage. You told us that Carl is abusive, Trish, but are you still choosing to stay with him?"

"Yes."

"Why, Trish?"

"I married Carl a year ago, he's my baby daddy, my son's father."

"Trish, I understand this is tough, and it's painful. And I know that Carl is of great significance in your life. I can imagine that you have all kinds of emotions, but we don't want him to hurt you anymore, do we? Or the kids."

Trish jumped in. "No one understands. I've got another baby and another baby daddy. I was married before. I divorced my first baby daddy. I would bring shame on my family if I split again. Twice—I can't do that. And Carl is my brother's best friend, Phyllis. A friend of the family."

I stayed expressionless. I needed time to think; to say something that would resonate with Trish and the others. You could feel the tension in a room of women who were crying out for help, waiting for a response from their mentor.

A minute passed before I spoke.

"Trish, if Carl is hurting you, it's not good for you, and it's certainly not good for the kids. His violence is likely to escalate. And it will wear you down until you can no longer function. It's toxic; poison for the soul. The physical scars will heal, but the emotional scars live on."

"You suffer. The kids suffer. They lose their childhood and eventually they won't feel loved and will blame themselves for these violent events. They could suffer huge insecurities and difficulties throughout their lives."

"You are all experiencing trauma, honey."

"Kids need a healthy home and a good role model in order to do well. This is about you, Trish, but it's also about the future of your children. Can we work on your situation a bit today? I would like to . . ."

But as my words trailed off, Trish began screaming.

"No! No! Never. I can't. I can't go through this again. I can't shame my family. I need to stay with Carl. He was wonderful to me until . . . until we got married. Maybe . . . someday . . . not now."

I'm thinking: damn this shame thing. Futures are in the balance. I need to reach Trish.

Trish explained that while she was in prison, the children were temporarily safe in care of her mom. Although that was comforting, I was extremely concerned about her return to an abuser. She was scheduled to be released in 15 days and, at first, she would be on probation.

But I had an ace. Trish's mom. If she was caring for the kids, it meant she was well-intended, supportive and capable. Hopefully.

"Trish, I understand. I understand that you don't want to bring shame on your family. Shame is awkward and it's painful. I also understand exactly why you want to stay with Carl. I, too, married someone once just to make my dad happy and ended up with three mortgages, two kids and a vacuum cleaner. It sucked."

There was a snicker in the room.

"Trish, I wonder if we could do a simple group exercise. It might clarify a few things for you, and we can all learn something today. Would that be okay?"

I was flying on instinct and hoping to influence a troubled young mom. Trish nodded. As she was resisting change she was screaming for help. Acknowledging the problem was a launch pad.

Fingers crossed everyone we're cleared for takeoff!

Fortunately, we'd been studying relationship health for weeks. So before Trish could change her mind, I ripped a sheet from my notepad and instructed the ladies to write down one important quality that a partner must possess in order to maintain a wholesome relationship.

"Ladies, could each of you please list a relationship essential, something you value in a healthy relationship." They were instructed to pass the paper around the room.

Here's what the ladies wrote:

Honesty	Love
Trust	Intelligent
Tells the truth	Responsibility
Funny	Likes my kids
Smart	Gentle
Supports me	Kindness
	Reasonable and Fair

I reviewed the list, added "Reasonable and Fair," and then handed it to Trish.

"Trish, please review the list carefully. Place a checkmark where Carl possesses the quality. And where Carl does not possess the quality, cross it off."

With fierce concentration, Trish reviewed the list. After several moments, she lifted her pencil and forcefully drew two or three heavy black lines through every value. It was as if she was releasing her anger. And that was good.

Then Trish gently placed the pencil in front of her and handed the paper back to me. There was silence. Trish seemed calm, but my anxiety was soaring. Slowly, I turned to Trish and pleaded for her life.

"Great work, Trish, great!" I looked at the sheet of paper.

"Trish, look at this discovery. Carl possesses none of the qualities that we need to succeed in a healthy relationship. All of the good stuff that we've talked about—you've crossed off. All of it."

"Yes," Trish confirmed softly, "I know."

"Perhaps Carl once had these qualities, Trish, but people change. Stress changes us and sometimes it's not so good. You have nothing to feel ashamed of Trish. Nothing at all."

I was forming a mental bridge to wellness. I needed to take Trish from where she began to a place where she was free of Carl, with family support. Perhaps it was working.

"Isn't it possible, Trish, that maybe your family would understand? That your brother would want a better life for you and a better life for his niece and nephew?"

Dear Universe, please help.

"I don't know," she said.

That's a breakthrough. We started at "never."

"Trish, I am sad to hear about your struggle with Carl. Sad for you and sad for the kids. I don't believe that those who love you want this for you. Your family doesn't know what Carl is doing. And none of us know what Carl is capable of doing.

"In fact, isn't it possible that your mom is worried about all of you? Couldn't she even be hoping you leave Carl? Seeing your daughter in prison changes stuff for a mom. This has to be painful for her too."

"It's possible," she said quietly looking into her lap.

"Trish, I care about you. Look around the room, we all care. We would never judge you. My role is to encourage goodness in you and for you. Do you trust me?"

She nodded and began to sob. At this point, more ladies were crying than not. And I'm the biggest suck in the room. "Honey, your life is important. Your life matters. It must have value, and it must have meaning. You are returning to a toxic environment. An environment that's dangerous for you and for your children.

"There's no excuse for abuse. And this threatening situation at home could land you in prison again. If things go wrong, you could be doing significantly more jail time. And that would leave your kids without a mom.

"As a first time offender, your sentence was light. But, the next sentence . . . There's even a chance you could lose custody of the kids. We know that physical abuse escalates.

"In my opinion, there's a very real concern that Carl might hurt the kids. The situation could go from critical to fatal. We never know. Carl has already caused emotional damage. What can we do, Trish?"

We were breathing in unison now. After a long pause, Trish glanced at me and away. Slowly, she looked around the room, one lady at a time, as if she needed an expression of support. We all felt the gravity of the moment.

I was tense. Patience is tough—silence, tougher.

"Okay," she whispered with a dimpled half-smile.

The women sighed in relief. Everyone cared.

"I'll call my lawyer in the morning."

The following week, Trish shared that she had called her lawyer and that he was preparing divorce papers. She went on to say that she had spoken with her mom and explained the work we had done in class. She asked for understanding and support, and Mom offered to pay for the lawyer and assist in the transition. Trish and the kids would be living with her mom. And Mom had been hoping for this.

Trish received a gift with her prison sentence. Had she not been incarcerated, who knows what might have happened.

Now Trish would have her freedom. This didn't mean that life would be easy, but divorce was an opportunity to heal and a chance to rebuild.

In my work, I believe that I reach some people in each audience. My messages are often remembered and sometimes they make a difference. I call that a counsellor's prayer.

Despite physical abuse and a prison cell, Trish hesitated to leave her husband out of shame. I realized then, in many ways, I was Trish. That was my marriage: a habit, a convenience and shameful to leave.

Later, exhausted from the emotional work with Trish that afternoon, I slumped over the steering wheel in my car. I admitted for the first time: You don't have a healthy relationship either. I had simply been carrying on, not recognizing that I had created a life of my own within the marriage, but the marriage itself was unfulfilling and I had overlooked too much for too long. When we get a wakeup call, we must wake up.

It was time to walk the walk.

That evening, I went home and asked Philip, my second husband, for a divorce. I'd spent twenty years with the wrong guy.

How did I get here?

Years ago, during my first marriage (to Lenny), I was working part time for a lawyer. Allen Weinstein was a round, lovable, neighbourhood practitioner who was addicted to vursht (salami) and frequently had a bright yellow drop of French's Mustard on his moustache. Successful and demanding, Allen hired me to be his litigation clerk. I was fond of Allen and his overzealous clients were fun too.

I had just interviewed a divorce petitioner one morning when my husband Lenny called to say hello and, shockingly, added goodbye. After 11 years, two kids and a colour TV, Lenny decided that he had married too young. Who could argue with that? He gently explained that he wanted to play the field. And Lenny was right. We were just wrong.

Lenny rented a nearby apartment, packed up his stereo and would be in touch when he wanted to borrow the vacuum cleaner. It seemed reasonable, except that there was no mention of child support. Lenny was bankrupt.

At ages two and five, the kids couldn't understand the implications of divorce. And frankly, neither could I. Notwithstanding, Lenny and I remained friends as I handed him a divorce on the grounds of adultery. Lenny had found a new princess and married her two days after divorcing me. Mazel tov.

So there I was, barely thirty, with two toddlers and a part-time job. It's amazing how macaroni and cheese can become an art form. Still, I was excited about the prospects of being sexy and single. To be honest, though, sexy needed some work.

After a short cry and a deep breath, I marched myself into Allen's office, shut the door and told him we had a problem. Reluctantly, I explained the Lenny thing and resigned from my position. I needed to secure a full time job to pay the bills.

Without hesitation, Allen rose from his desk, excused himself and fired his real estate clerk. Within minutes, Allen offered me the clerk job. I had absolutely no real estate experience, but Allen said, "I'll teach you."

That week, I hired a nanny, began my new job and started a diet. I was starving myself in readiness for dating and truly excited about picking out my next husband. But hey, that's me: resilient.

Five months later, fifty pounds lighter, and determined to develop a romantic profile, I began to date. With no dating skills, I approached this task like a serious job hunt. You create a checklist and then set out to find the "man" who checks the most boxes. Simple.

Not so much. A dozen years later, having experimented with several men, I found Mr. Little Italy. And that was Philip, otherwise known as husband number two.

Some couples never have sex and are deliriously happy. There is no normal or healthy level of sexual desire or activity. If it's working for both parties, there's nothing to sweat over. However, a sexless marriage can be anguish if the wrong people are involved.

Philip was a very nice man, but celibacy was never my plan.

After a dozen years of abstinence and a heroic effort to save my marriage, I decided that nice wasn't good enough anymore. After that agonizing day of working with Trish, I headed home to fix Philip.

"Philip, can we talk please?"

He knew my tone had a purpose. "Sure thing."

"Our marriage needs help. It seriously needs fixing. We need counselling, Philip," I said, expecting him to say 'sure thing.'

But he didn't. "What?" he said, confused. "Why?"

Clearly, he had no idea what was wrong. We had always gotten along beautifully. In the absence of communication, there was peace. I had a career that defined me and family and friends who loved me. Add the fulfillment of volunteerism and who needs a husband? I kept myself so immersed in appreciation and ice cream that I never paused long enough to realize what I was missing.

Until Trish.

Like her, I thought I couldn't face a second divorce. I'd created a private world where I carried on without examining my marriage or working for a deeper partnering experience.

"I want to bring intimacy back into our relationship," I announced.

And he looked at me like he'd seen a ghost.

"We don't need a counsellor, you need a counsellor," he bellowed in a tone I had never heard.

"What's wrong with our marriage?"

"We have no intimacy," I pleaded, syllable by syllable.

It was awkward. A serious argument about sex ensued and then Philip said the fatal words.

"You have a problem. Not me. I'm happy in this marriage. I'm happy exactly the way things are. You need a psychiatrist, not me."

I had expected more of him. In a relationship when one person has a problem, both have a problem. My head and my heart were screaming in unison now: "Get the hell out. It's time."

I calmly said, "We'll get a divorce." I heard myself say that like one might say, "I'll make lamb."

Now, let's be clear, couples who choose not to have physical intimacy can still enjoy a full and satisfying relationship.

But I wasn't one of those gals. Despite facing tremendous personal pain and financial destruction, Philip lacked the backbone to speak up. Weeks after he left the house, I found a note he had tucked away. It was scribbled with the name and number of a suicide hotline. But Philip had never uttered a word of regret, nor did he ever hint that he wanted me to stay.

And so I traded 3,500 fabulously appointed square feet for uncertainty, fear and a rented basement apartment—and began anew. By this time, my kids were married and quite grown up.

Mom was still finding her way.

CHAPTER NINETEEN

Third time is a charm

BUT WAIT, there's more!

After encouraging Trish to leave her husband, I was inspired to leave mine. Second husband once removed, I finally began to see life as fleeting. I had spent far too long coasting on disappointment.

Being decisive is good, though. When I commit to moving forward, I don't indulge in doubt that doesn't serve me. I find it far better to fuck up and fix it than do nothing at all.

So, I gave myself a year to find love. I decided if Mother Earth could orbit the sun in 365 days, I could focus every fibre of my being on matters of the heart.

A little over sixty and single all of two hours, I signed myself on to Plenty of Fish, a dating website. I wrote a profile that read somewhere between a law firm resume and a hooker's theme song and began the process. Oh sure, I had heard those scary stories about online dating, but I was anxious for tenderness.

For me, dating is a serious project. Finding your forever love is not a part-time job. Like any change worthy of the endeavour (and we are all worthy of love), it took a plan and execution to realize.

Thank you corporate Canada for giving me these great skills.

Remembering my mother's words, "Phyllis, anything worth having is worth working at," I became a serial dater. I went on seven dates a week. Every evening an interview opportunity unfolded. There were no pauses, no breaks and no weekends off. But as one date cascaded into the next, disappointment became a way of life. Either they lacked moral character, had unrealistic expectations of what surviving sixty looked like or hit my boredom limit in the first 30 minutes.

In fact, I actually found myself counselling most of these guys. Especially the ones who pretended to be single. I barely had enough time to sip my coffee before they'd arrogantly announce that they just might be a bit married. Who does that?

It happened twice.

Talk about fakery, one of these married guys left his chariot at home to ride in on a red hot motorcycle. This ethic-free alien actually had the nerve to tell me that he had both a wife and a mistress, and I was auditioning for third place. So, at a luncheon diner on Highway 7, Gary received my counsel that afternoon. It was worth far more than what he'd paid for my humble Greek salad and black coffee.

It was challenging to reach Gary, though, because he was convinced that his "high profile" mistress was worth far more than a "tiresome old marriage." I found Gary repulsive and exhausting.

Some of the single "fish members" weren't much better. Stanley was a widower who'd agreed to meet me at a coffee shop on a Saturday afternoon. I prettied up and drove myself to Dunkin' Donuts. It was a long drive for a short date.

As I was rotating in through the turnstile door, I recognized Stanley rotating out. (We had seen one another's profile pictures.) So, I circled back out to the sidewalk and asked if he was, in fact, Sir Stanley.

"Yes, I am," he said, as if leaving without meeting me somehow complied with dating etiquette.

"I'm Phyllis!" I announced, like it was important.

"I know," he admitted, looking away, "I saw you coming."

Stanley had been peering through the café windows into the parking lot, in an effort to assess my wife-worthiness.

"Are we having coffee this afternoon, Stanley?" I asked foolishly as he peered at me with his keys jangling.

"No," he said. "I just had one."

"So, you're leaving without a word?"

"Yes, I'm leaving. You look nothing like my late wife."

He was actually angry with me and eager to tell me why. He explained that he had driven in from some faraway place, and I wasn't worth the gas. So I apologized, got into my car and screamed a little. Then I looked in the mirror and told myself I was okay. Stanley—not so much. But there I was, dressed my best with no place to go. I had made myself single and was beginning to wonder why.

I did send Stanley a lengthy text message with a full cheat sheet on dating etiquette. The teacher in me made me do it. I explained that although I had confidence in myself and was not emotionally crushed by his brutal rejection, another woman might be. And that would be cruel.

Stanley wrote back: "sure"—with no capital "S" and no punctuation. The very definition of a schmuck.

Being single after years of coupledom is scary. But courage has its rewards. A year later, with a more flattering picture, glorious makeup and help from my fairy godmother, I met John. Even with our long distance challenges and insanely busy lives, it was magical. But more on John later.

I must emphasize here that I'm not advocating for anyone to give up their relationship and head to the internet. We have an obligation to ourselves and our partners to try saving a viable relationship first.

Are you in one that's chock full of love, appreciation and harmony? Or do you wish that things could be different? As a student of life, I would like to offer these relationship tips to enhance your happily-ever-after odds.

Even the strongest relationship will have difficult days. For best results, combine commitment, compromise and communication and then generously add affection, as required. With motivation, good intentions and hard work, it is possible to rekindle our relationships and reignite our lives.

Does your person make you feel loved?

There's a distinction between being loved and feeling loved, with a far greater value on feeling. After all, what's the use of being loved if you don't feel it? Feeling loved involves being accepted and valued for who we are. We can't expect any relationship to operate on autopilot. These puppies need regular attention. Designate a space free of devices, and make your time together matter.

Emotional intimacy is fundamental to a thriving relationship. Without it, you create distance. I advise couples to do a relationship audit about every six months. Some couples never pause long enough to smell the roses in their relationship and then wonder how their Garden of Eden grew such thick weeds.

Lying is strictly forbidden, as is lying by omission. Withholding information with the intention of hiding the truth is lying too. These culprits erode trust and damage relationships before you can shout, "I'll explain!"

In a healthy relationship, each person must have a safe space to express their concerns without fear of retaliation. While some couples use their quiet voices to discuss differences, others disagree with intense passion (like me, of course). No party should fear conflict because conflict serves a positive purpose.

Conflict signals a need for change and forces us to assess. The key to conflict resolution is determining the end goal and then approaching our person with respect and kindness. Sadly, I spent twenty years avoiding conflict, and all it got me was a basement apartment and a few nice plants.

We can't expect that any one person will satisfy our full spectrum of needs. That's called 'needy.' If we expect all of our stars to shine from the same galaxy, it puts way too much pressure on that galaxy. The stars will dim and the relationship will die.

Have you noticed that falling in love happens organically, but preserving it requires attention? The Righteous Brothers sing about it in "You've Lost That Lovin' Feelin'." Their lyrics describe what happens when we stop working on the relationship or the relationship stops working for us.

Which brings us to communication.

Picture this: an argument happens and you say nothing, but actually you're speaking volumes. Nonverbal cues like eye rolling, posturing and positioning can make for a shit hot mess. Matching our body language with our words is critical for building trust. Positive actions like leaning in, eye contact and hand touching are gestures that can often communicate more effectively than words. In fact, a warm and understanding nod can be much more effective than a whole speech.

After studying neuro-linguistic programming for years, I praise the power of body language. Being aware of our nonverbal cues—and interpreting others'— is imperative for effective communication. It helps us better understand a situation and the feelings involved.

When a couple feels confident in their intimate connection, the relationship is at peace. When couples stop communicating, this disconnect precipitates an epic fail. Keep the communication strong, ask your partner for exactly what you need and get granular. Sometimes a small detail inspires a big solution. For some of us, asking for something is difficult. It makes us feel awkward, embarrassed or even ashamed. I urge you to be mindful that providing comfort to someone you love is a pleasure, not a problem. And working through a problem together elevates closeness.

When I mess up badly I steer clear of defending, dismissing, or denying. I try to understand how my craziness affects his craziness. A bit of empathy goes a long way toward smoothing out a situation.

Another essential is the ability to listen. Active listening is couple glue. A good listener will listen with emotion and focus on what the other person is saying without distraction, objection or interruption. Challenging, right? But that's what makes your partner feel respected rather than rejected. And it lessens the tension.

A rather frustrated husband (not one of mine) once told me that the day his wife actually listened to his point of view, he marked the calendar and opened a bottle of champagne.

But, and it's a big one, being a good listener does not mean agreeing with all you hear. With a difference of opinion, honesty is crucial—but delivered softly and gently. Not everything needs to be said. And I have found that thinking before I speak is also helpful. Stating an opinion respectfully is a learned skill. However, once mastered, the ability to discuss differences with respect and kindness is a boost and a must.

Make an effort to spend time together. My friend Sherry Clodman smiles as she describes that she and her husband Joel, married more than twenty years, take turns planning an exciting date night activity. They even find fun in the planning. Essential, though, is their motivation to make the time count and a desire to express their love.

New experiences keep a relationship fresh, but it doesn't have to be a trip to Tahiti. For a wonderful bonding experience, try a new restaurant, a new part of town or an elaborate picnic for two on a secluded lake. Clothing optional.

I recall my honeymoon in Italy. We were on a secluded beach that inspired me to get physical. Philip didn't put up much of a fuss that day but by the time he prepared himself for sex by building a private, well-constructed, non-flammable, safe and secure hut with a sharp pocketknife and some soggy driftwood, the moment had passed. Philip was a terrific handyman but his sexual partnering was much less exciting. Ah, looking back—the clues are always there.

A powerful path to increasing connection is focusing on a cause. Humans are hardwired to lend a hand. Doing things together that benefit others creates pride and generates significant pleasure. The more we help, the happier we are and this is true for singles and couples.

Each of us is a co-creator in our relationships. How do you want your story to read? Learning to recognize the root source of our anger and using techniques to calm ourselves will lessen the need for damage control.

Let's take a moment to consider affection. The human touch is an essential part of our existence. Infants need constant affection and cuddling for healthy brain development. And the benefits don't end in childhood. Sexting and other forms of digital messaging are great for rhymes and mimes, but fail to stimulate the nervous system to release testosterone, estrogen, dopamine and oxytocin.

A personal computer can't replace a personal encounter.

As important as sex can be for the health of a relationship, it's not the only form of physical intimacy that registers in the brain and promotes wellbeing. Holding hands, hugging and kissing are all shown to produce an equal or greater amount of oxytocin—the chemical that does so much for so many. It reduces stress and inflammation, improves wound healing, lessens cravings and lowers heart rates.

Focusing on our relationship is not reserved for the worst of times. Practising continuous care encourages the best of times.

CHAPTER TWENTY

Let's make love

S O, GARY WAS MARRIED and Stanley left me at the coffee shop altar. After completing an eleven month dating circus, I had begun to wonder if I needed a new hairdo, brighter lipstick or a revised plan.

But later that evening, I received a "fish" message through the dating website:

"Hi, I'm John. You looked at my profile but passed me by without so much as a note. Perhaps I live too far away. Shall we see?"

His face was gorgeous, and his profile was brilliant, but he was right, John was three hours away by car. How could it work?

"Yes, you live too far . . . no plans to move," I wrote.

"Why don't we phone chat just to rule it out?"

"Sure, call me." And I left my number.

John wrote back that he would call at 8 p.m. and I was flattered.

At precisely 8 p.m., I received a note that said: "I'm currently in rehearsal, please give me a bit more time. I have not forgotten about you. I will call as soon as I arrive home."

And I'm thinking: This can't be true. A guy who keeps his word. And what rehearsal?

An hour later, John called and we talked for ages. It was a casual conversation with no agenda—it felt like an old friend or a new comforter. We shared our joys and sorrows, our accomplishments and failures. Our conversation was deep and meaningful. There was even a mild mutual flirtation that created intrigue and sparked my excitement. Oh, for the joy of chemistry!

As we shared our lives that first talk, John gave me an open, vulnerable account of how he remained married for thirty years to a woman who struggled with alcohol addiction. He shared his countless attempts to "fix" her, his painful disappointments and how a dysfunctional family survived in secrecy.

I described my two failed marriages and my quest for romantic permanence. Neither of us wanted to play games. I told him about my prison work, which intrigued John, a fellow volunteer enthusiast.

Then, I made it clear that I could never move. Being distanced from my children was untenable. As a result, getting together would only be viable if John was open to relocating in Toronto. He explained that he was committed to a theatre group in Haliburton, but when the performances ended, he could relocate. This was not an agreement, nor was it a promise. It was simply our first phone call. But the conversation was serious enough to explore the possibility of a life together without ever using those words.

As evening turned into morning, I fell asleep with the phone in my lap and a text message that read: "I will call you tomorrow."

I liked that.

I was so excited to be receiving call number two that evening that I could think of little else. But by 9 p.m., there was no call. Saddened but prepared for disappointment, I texted John as follows: "Change of Heart?"

The phone rang and we spoke for hours.

I was captivated by John's intelligence, humour and extraordinary humanity. I wondered if you could fall in love over a phone call. Or if I'd lost my sanity.

The nightly phone calls continued for weeks until we decided to end the mystery and meet in person. John invited me to lunch at a fish restaurant near me. I told him I'd meet him there. I was serious about meeting this man, but that was no excuse to drop the security dating measures that are especially important to women.

But a few days before our scheduled date, I changed my mind. A woman's birthright. That evening when John called and jokingly asked if I was ready to meet him, I announced that I would not be meeting him for lunch. There was a long pause, and I understood that he might be disappointed.

"I don't want fish," I announced firmly. "I want to see you, all of you. I need to know where you live and how you live. So guess who's coming to dinner, John? I'm coming to Haliburton, and I shall be there on Saturday at six."

There was a long pause. He had either dropped the line or just dropped. Much later, John explained that he had actually held the phone up and looked at it questioningly, unsure if he had heard me properly.

He was shocked. The nerve of this woman. Or was it courage? My behaviour set the relationship tone. It also spoke of a life of determination.

"You get in life what you have the courage to ask for," says Oprah.

Haliburton in winter offers scarce hotel or restaurant choices. Difficult to stage a romance, but I was on a serious mission. A Google search turned up the Silver Maple Motel, a seedy spot in town—actually, the only motel in town operating in November. It was no place for a classy woman, but why would I care? And the nearby coffee shop could be an asset.

Before I left that Saturday, a violent snowstorm rolled in. It was unnerving. I started to think that the universe was telling me to stay put or that my father, the hellion from heaven, was being cruel. Dad would never have approved of this field trip.

I have no idea how I made it to Haliburton but, after hours of driving in snow motion, I reached town an exhausted frazzle. John was to pick me up in an hour, but the party girl was running on fumes. I sent him a text that read: "I'm here but exhausted. Let's meet in the morning."

And he said: "I'll be there in ten minutes."

The storm never did let up. By the time John arrived at Motel Six, I looked good and felt bad. Until I saw him. When I opened the door, China blue eyes pierced my heart. Alive and alert once again, I was excited to begin.

Oh my God, he was a whole buffet of fine. Adorable and irresistible in blue jeans and a tight blue sweater that matched his eyes, he had silvery hair. Casual but captivating.

John was a head taller than me with a strong enough build for a wrap-around hug. The very thing that had been missing for years. I still remember our enchanting first hug.

Explaining that there are no winter restaurants in cottage country, John suggested we settle for the coffee shop diner. Chili never tasted so good. We sat in two comfy fireside chairs and chatted easily. A relief from the stormy weather. John was a very attractive man who was void of arrogance and full of charm. He seemed unaware of his physical attributes. He was friendly, flirty and quite fabulous.

It was November, coming on Christmastime. The holiday décor and cozy feeling made for a romantic setting. After hours of coffee and donut dialogue, we drove back to my motel. Neither of us wanted the evening to end.

I invited John into my room, but it wasn't until we entered that I realized there were no chairs. This freezing cold motel room had a door that opened to a double bed and a single sink. I remember thinking, ironically, it wasn't much more than a jail cell. But nothing mattered.

As we sat on the bed cross-legged and across from one another, we continued to swap personal stories and lifelong goals. But before long, the mood evolved from energy to Eros. Hesitancy faded. Before that night, I had gone a dozen years without ever having a hug.

John and I awoke the next morning to celebrate our meeting and a memorable date. And so it began, with breakfast at Kosy Korner, a small country kitchen on Haliburton's main drag.

Falling in love was easy. But it would be months before John's theatre contract was finished. Drawn to one another, we began commuting between Haliburton and Toronto in the dead of winter with storms, schedules and unpleasant surprises often keeping us apart. I attended all of his rehearsals and even snuck him into a prison gig once. Each time we said goodbye, I was gripped by his absence, missing him before he'd pulled out of the driveway.

John never missed a chance to visit.

One day he was speaking about the homeless problem in Haliburton, explaining that some of the money raised by his theatre company would go towards feeding and heating the homeless and needy.

That got me thinking. I wondered if we could coordinate a homeless holiday dinner. John's enthusiasm surpassed mine. That month we collected vegetables from local farmers, had meats donated by nearby restaurants and arranged for the church to open their basement and include Bill the organist. Everyone loved big Bill.

John did the cooking, I peeled the carrots and the church ladies baked some cake. It was a wonderful day in the neighbourhood. Tummies were full, smiles were contagious and emotions were high.

The winter flew by. But, here's a question: How do we stay in love once we fall in love?

Let's start with sex.

Is sex still electrifying your relationship? Or has sexual desire decreased over time so that sex is now more of an obligation than an aspiration?

The start of a relationship can be quite intoxicating. Everything is exciting as we experience pleasure from a simple chat or a dinner for two. Firsts are fabulous and the initial stages of physical attraction are exhilarating. But physical attraction can take us only so far. Of greater importance is what we learn about the person through experience. As we begin to observe our partner's behaviour toward us and others, more mature feelings and emotional connection take root.

With sexual intimacy, all roads lead to the mind. Our brains are involved in all aspects of sexual behaviour from desire to arousal to orgasm and after play. Good physical intimacy requires trust and vulnerability. When you add these components to love and respect, you get connection and creativity without the fear of embarrassment or disappointment.

Sexual intimacy happens when people engage in sensual or sexual activities. A variety of physical techniques in concert with, or in place of, sexual intercourse can pave the path to paradise. Creativity and the freedom to explore one another with knowledge and consent defines a healthy sex life.

In intimate relationships, there will typically be one person with more desire than the other. Communication is key, both in and out of the bedroom. If a healthy love life is important to you, speaking about it is too. Healthy intimacy involves parties willing to take the initiative and ask for such closeness. It's only fair to share the vulnerability. A sex request carries the risk of rejection.

Esther Perel, a well-known psychotherapist specializing in relationships, put it brilliantly: "Sex is not something you do. It's a place you go." As organic as intimacy is for some couples, others struggle to develop it, and struggle harder to maintain it. In Perel's work on the difference between sexuality and eroticism, she points out that when it comes to sexuality, there's a distinction between animals and humans.

While animals have sex to satisfy a procreative urge, humans have a more erotic interest in love-making. Sex offers an expression of freedom. It provides pleasure for the sake of pleasure. It brings vibrancy and vitality into our lives and allows for playfulness, curiosity, mystery and transcendence.

I see eroticism as a source of light, lust and excitement. If love makes the world go round, then eroticism rocks it.

Communication is to sex what toppings are to pizza. Everyone wants a pie, but toppings vary and need to be discussed! As our tastes evolve, so must our communication. The more open and often we communicate, the better we play.

A serious chat about love-making indicates a clear interest in the physical side of your relationships and brings you closer. Wondering about intimacy is not an option. Discuss your sexual preferences both at the cognitive level (before the games begin) and at the active level (game on). Otherwise, your shyness or inability to direct traffic may leave you both stuck.

I recognize that talking about sex may be awkward and agonizing for some people. If so, try writing or messaging your thoughts. I'm not kidding. Though texting is a less desirable way of communicating, it's better than nothing at all. No one is a mind reader. It you don't let your partner know what your fantasies are, you will just be having maintenance sex. "All function no fantasy" diminishes the shine over time.

For most couples, intimacy is also significantly affected by stress. Stress is seldom a good thing, but for sexual maintenance we should distinguish between short term and long term stressors.

When someone loses their job or is tending a serious illness, intimacy is often the first to go. If you are experiencing long term stress or anxiety, be open with your partner. A warm heart and a shoulder to lean on are a welcome pair for de-stressing and seeking solutions. Be patient and try to ensure that you make time for one another, even if it's just morning coffee. Recognize that chronic stress is complicated and may require counselling.

Sex drives will fluctuate. Cuddles and kisses are even more important during a low tide. Accept that it may take a bit more time and attention for a happy love-making experience. Or decide to postpone for a bit. Developing intimacy takes work, but the effort we make today becomes the bond we share tomorrow.

When your partner does something nice, express yourself. Everybody likes to be shown they're special and that they add something wonderful to your life. Even simple compliments will build better bonds.

Every relationship goes through good and bad times. Life is navigating through challenges that will affect your relationship and test your better angels. So, flexibility, resiliency and tolerance are the skills to master.

Change is inevitable and the better we adapt to surprises, the happier we'll be.

Arguments cause frustration, resentment, anger and hurt feelings. And anger will kill a passionate evening faster than a fire alarm. If you spend the day fighting, it's unlikely you'll spend the night loving. It's tough hugging a porcupine. If arguing has become the new norm, seek counselling. Changing a single step can change the entire dance.

When you think of intimacy, do you think only of sensual pleasures? Intimacy is an affectionate relationship that goes beyond sexual intercourse. Intimacy is about closeness, quality time, and creating and maintaining a healthy relationship.

Amen.

CHAPTER TWENTY-ONE

Seniors who sizzle

WHEN JOHN AND I MET we were both in our sixties. He came to me on a winter's breeze, warmed my heart, renewed my romantic faith and then went home. But one thing is clear, I never have to coax him under the covers or over the moon. And when we hug, he looks at me like I gave him a freaking gift.

It's a myth that sexual intimacy has a cut-off date. Sex therapists agree that interest in, and the capacity for, sex continues into our eighties. Sure, it may decrease in intensity but not necessarily. As I write this chapter, it occurs to me that my adult children will be reading this and likely feeling rather ill. Read on kids, you'll get there too.

By the time John moved to Toronto, we had rented a basement apartment and moved in together, but fussy folk questioned my sanity.

"Basement?" they bantered as if it were a socially forbidden class. One friend actually felt justified in ending our friendship, advising that my behaviour was completely reckless. God, I was tempted to tell her she was an alte kaker (crotchety old timer).

For the first time in my life, I truly didn't care what others thought. We were happy in our basement for three years that flew by. Then we purchased a lovely condo, furnished it in Phyllis fashion and threw a party.

John is the love of my life, but it's not always magic and sweet magnolias. We struggle too. We bicker, we banter and there's drama. But the love is strong, and we have a remarkably safe space to work out our issues with respect and kindness. Most importantly, I trust him with my heart.

Just before moving into the condo, I planned John's birthday dinner at our favourite spot, Peter's Fine Dining. We love the romantic feel of an authentic eighties-style eatery, its waiters and its traditional fare. It takes cozy a notch higher and the food is divine.

After dinner, I noticed that John was a bit distracted. And when he started using his cell phone, it triggered my agitation. A moment later, my phone buzzed—a message from John:

"I'm on one knee . . ."

That evening, with a full complement of waiters and diners around us, a grown man got down on one knee with a tiny ring box, a heart of gold and a gorgeous smile. We became engaged as the crowd applauded. And we remain extraordinarily happy.

Do we plan to marry?

Yes. We want to applaud life and showcase love. Whether the lights are on or off, we recognize our oneness and interconnectedness. Although we may have stray greys, it's not over till it's over. Sexual fitness is important at any age, and we don't outgrow our desire for sexual intimacy. It may not be the same as it was in our youth, but it can still be a ride you won't want to miss.

What I found after several months of dating is that all men are not created equally, but they do have something in common. I was always assured that if and when I might be "interested" they would surely stand at attention—no matter what it took to get there. It was life affirming.

I remember Danny the serial dater rather well. I thought we might have a lot in common because he was a criminal lawyer. Danny prided himself on his little red car and big black book. While some men collected technical gadgets, Danny was collecting ladies. He was definitely interesting. After treating me to an hour of his company and a slice of pot pie, Danny offered his services. He explained that he was polyamorous and invited me to join his harem.

Danny was smart and lusty, but no judge of women. When I suggested that I preferred a dedicated guy, he said, "Why would I give up my crowd-pleasing activities to gamble on one lonely woman?" It was a rhetorical question and I was soon homeward bound. I didn't even bother coaching someone who could only be described as a creep.

To sustain satisfying sexual intimacy, open up. Talk openly and honestly. Make time to be sexual with one another and don't forget to flirt. Oh, you thought flirting was reserved for nightclubs? No. It begins in the head and ends in the bed. Seniors, we won't get physical at night if we don't plan well before lights out. And this would include some big communication and some little blue pills to encourage sexual success. Just one pill per night, please.

And safe sex is not just for the young at heart. If you're having sex with a new partner or various partners, carry a condom. Sexually transmitted diseases are a serious concern and seniors don't get a pass.

As we age, the challenges change. As women reach menopause, levels of the hormone estrogen decrease, which often leads to vaginal dryness and slower arousal. Women also experience emotional changes which may diminish our sexual appetite. Our body shape is also changing, which often causes us to feel less sexual or sexually desirable. On the plus side, aging allows women the freedom of physical intimacy without the worry of pregnancy.

As a man ages, it will likely take longer for his penis to become firm, stay firm, and reach orgasm. So listen up, men. This may not be your favourite topic but, for optimum health and wellness, please seek medical guidance and get back to work.

The testosterone hormone is male magic. Testosterone levels may vary at any age, but older men generally have less. Generally, levels decline gradually at a rate of about one percent per year after age thirty. Other medical challenges may affect testosterone too.

We all know that exercise has many health benefits. It encourages a healthy heart and weight and adds years to our lives. Exercise will also improve our sex lives. In fact, exercise helps us achieve our daily activities with greater ease and our sexual activities with greater satisfaction.

Now, please excuse me while I do my gentle push-ups.

Any condition that affects your general health may also affect your sexual health. Some conditions that involve the cardiovascular system, like high blood pressure, diabetes and hormone levels may challenge normal sexual function. The medications used to treat these conditions can have an effect as well. Speak with your doctor to see if your medication can be adjusted or another added to deal with an unwanted side effect.

If you're looking for reasons to get back in the saddle, research shows that sex: boosts the immune system, burns calories, lowers blood pressure, induces sleep, increases intimacy, is a natural relaxant and pain reliever, sharpens the mind, heightens self-esteem, reduces depression and anxiety and may even lessen the risk of heart attack and prostate cancer.

Just saying.

CHAPTER TWENTY-TWO

Different libidos

MANY COUPLES HAVE LIBIDOS that just don't jibe. When this happens, the relationship takes a hit. Trust me.

In the beginning, sex has the excitement that comes with novelty. But when our love-making goes from sizzle to fizzle, it could result in an unhealthy emotional cycle that requires a little something something.

Sexual intimacy bonds and comforts us in a security blanket of bliss. In fact, love-making creates a magnetic bond like no other. The goal therefore is shared pleasure that soothes the soul.

There are many physical and emotional factors that affect our sensuality and, therefore, our libido. Understandably, our sex drives will wane with physical challenges or emotional downturns. But if we enjoyed a healthy appetite before the difficult event, our hunger should return when the situation resolves.

When a high desire partner is constantly in hot pursuit of someone who'd rather be watching the news though, it's a problem. At first you will joke about it, but when the high desire partner must keep begging, both parties will grow frustrated. Even knowing that the rejection is not necessarily personal, it can still feel that way to those who must plead. They may even cheat to meet their needs.

Either partner may be more sexually pumped. This behaviour is not reserved for men and may bounce between the parties. But if mismatched desire has been the source of hurt feelings, angry talks or frequent frustration, a solution is crucial. If you're not working for a fix, you're worsening the problem.

Finding a compromise is key. I am not necessarily suggesting that you increase or decrease sexual traffic, but I do encourage all forms of physical and emotional intimacy. If you've tried your best and the relationship is still in trouble, seek sexual therapy or couples counselling for guidance.

The ability to communicate effectively is a dance of love, but, for some people, sex is a sensitive or awkward theme song. If you find this kind of talk touchy, stretch yourself a bit and have an adult conversation anyway. Even when there's nothing wrong, maintaining a healthy sex life still requires the occasional intimate chat, a check in, to ensure that both parties are good.

Silence is not always golden, nor is it a sign of contentment.

With crazy lives, we mark our calendars to ensure that important stuff happens. Sex is important stuff too. But when we're exhausted, sex is the last thing we need. So, find a time when you have the highest energy and the lowest distraction. Mark it down, make it happen, enjoy.

What makes us think sexy? Music, candles, red hot (or blue) movies? Pay attention to what gets you there and what does not. And then:

Bathe, groom, perfume.

Focus your intention on one another.

Think about the relationship appeal and charm.

Avoid distractions.

Dim the lights and make eye contact .

Imagine a warm encounter.

Did you know that we have both intercourse and outercourse? Don't forget about touch. Touch is a lovely way of saying "how much I love you." Holding hands is a great way of to maintain intimacy over the years. Kiss, cuddle, hug and hold hands. Your entire body has erotic possibilities. Explore.

And be spontaneous. Find a new place, another approach, or anything different to stimulate desire and inspire a different outcome. Take a shower together, or take back the couch or the floor or even the backyard. Simply talking about a sunny vacation may warm you up. So, google your dream destination and order up paradise for two. The planning and doing can do wonders for libido.

Now this is private, so please don't tell John. I discovered that when I play a video of him singing "You were Always on My Mind," my desire goes into overdrive. So now I play it from time to time. Accidentally. And only because I love music (ha!).

Okay, fasten your seatbelts, kids. Wikipedia defines sexting as sending, receiving, or forwarding sexually explicit messages, photographs, or videos, primarily between mobile phones.

I hope you can see the smile on my face.

There's science to support sexting as a relationship tool. Yes, sexting is said to increase intimate chatter and sexual activity. It improves relationship satisfaction for those with avoidance issues, such as failing to acknowledge feelings or handle emotional issues. Sending sexually explicit pictures also leads to an improved connection for those who suffer with attachment anxiety issues such as fear of rejection or abandonment.

So maybe it's time to get into the gutter. Just be careful, folks. It's important to know that the person you're sexting welcomes the call.

I once sent a text to a wrong number. Gus the bus driver was so flattered that he asked me out on a date. We never met, but I smile every time I think of my misdirected text: "Smoothing out a few wrinkles, be there soon."

If you've tried it all and frustration is overpowering an underachieving relationship, seek professional support. You'd be surprised how bedroom doors open after a few trips to your local sex therapist.

CHAPTER TWENTY-THREE

Shit happens

AT AGE FORTY, I still thought the best way to resolve an argument was by chasing my husband down a busy street while slowly removing my blouse. Although he looked back and smiled a bit, the conflict remained unresolved. Since then, I've come a very long way.

Conflict is never welcome. But shit happens, doesn't it?

In order for positive change to occur, we must manage conflict rather than avoid it. Constructive conflict management strengthens relationships.

Parties with incompatible goals fight, especially when two people believe only one can win. Typical difficulties may include any combination of these ingredients:

Poor Communication

Undemonstrated Appreciation

Undemonstrated Respect

Difficulty Compromising

Differing Priorities

Commitment

Lack of Support

Lack of Sensitivity

Lack of Compassion

Cultural Diversity

Hurtful Acts (intentional or unintentional)

Weak Emotional Connection

Weak Relationship

Betrayal

Infidelity

Resolving conflict successfully requires excellent communication skills which include honesty, vulnerability, empathy, compassion, and compromise. Can you bring it?

Navigating conflict frequently requires timing. I have to admit I'm still practising the "time out" specialty, but I have discovered a few timing advantages. I learned recently that the best time to resolve a conflict isn't always now and that perhaps we need a cooling off period, (geez how cold must it get). Seriously though, a timeout helps avoid saying or doing something we might regret and gives us a chance to identify the real issues.

During a time out, we may realize that the conflict wasn't really about the movie pick. It's likely something much deeper with ourselves personally or the relationship itself. Identifying the underlying cause of the upset will promote a more productive conversation and a permanent resolution.

Also, resolving conflict requires acceptance. When you chose a partner, you choose a whole set of unchangeable specifications. Emotional intelligence helps you accept your partner rather than try to change him or her. Counsellors joke that partners drop their spouses off on the therapist's couch and expect them to magically create change. Insisting that your partner do their thing your way is like asking a chicken to bark.

When issues arise, you have to decide whether it's a battle worth picking. I have a five-minute rule: if it won't matter in five minutes, for gosh sakes, let it go. If it won't matter in five weeks, we can let that go, too. But if it will impact the next five months or years, then that's when we go to the wall. Even then, using gentle language and the great respect will win the battle and nurse the soul.

It's also worth pointing out that the five-minute rule works best in conjunction with the "say less, listen more" rule.

Do you keep fighting only to remain stuck? That's where a clear message is essential. It contains a respectful but direct expression of what you fear and feel. Talking about your fear invokes empathy and connection. Talking about what you feel takes the emphasis off the wrong-doing and places it on what you or the relationship need for secure attachment.

An attack by checklist promotes defensiveness and ensures escalation. Focus on resolving one (or maybe two) important concerns and try not to go off script. Rome wasn't built in a day.

Rather than arguing about the less important bits, remember that it's okay to disagree. For more complex situations, combine communication with compassion to negotiate a compromise that works. There is almost nothing we can't resolve when two people are committed to oneness.

In conflict, a "win-win" is where the relationship wins, rather than any one person. This is critical and cannot be overstated. Ask yourself: Is what I'm about to say going to increase my chances of working out the problem or cause a greater divide?

Your end goal must drive every word and every action, so be a good listener. A good listener is a good partner. Active listening allows your partner to speak without interruption (a challenge). It's a focus on what is said rather than formulating a response. This step also helps to prevent further misunderstandings.

With every successful resolution, we become hopeful for a better tomorrow. Even the effort to resolve a conflict with dignity signals that both parties have the skills to resolve their differences and are invested in the relationship. Success reinforces the principle that with commitment, communication and compromise, everyone wins.

What about abuse?

There is a strong distinction between conflict and abuse. Abuse is not about love; it's about power and control. Abuse has no place in an intimate relationship. Therefore, there's no reason to stay. Abuse will damage your body and destroy your soul. I urge you to put yourself first and leave the relationship as soon as it's safe to do so, because abuse has no end date.

I have heard too many whispers from men and women who have earned themselves a prison stay because they could "handle it." If you are experiencing an unfair use of power, or any form of abuse, don't suffer in silence.

I remember Cathy the cashier. Cathy was desperate to explain that she found herself in prison one day because Carlos demanded she drive the getaway car he used for drug deals. Not only did that get her prison time, she came close to losing her life. A nervous addict pulled a gun on them, but somehow, miraculously, the gun was not loaded. That day, the universe stepped up.

We all have a past, but some people have suffered unthinkable abuse. When someone has been traumatized, they hold a memory of these events in their brains and in their bodies. That memory is often expressed in post-traumatic stress disorder symptoms such as nightmares, flashbacks and dissociative behaviours.

Trapped in unhappy and unhealthy?

If you're frustrated, lonely and miserable in your relationship, there's no shame in the game.

Walk away to peace and tranquility, knowing you've done all that you can.

CHAPTER TWENTY-FOUR

Effing around

J ACK AND JILL WENT UP the hill to . . . Wait! What?

Committing adultery is one of the ultimate betrayals. It plagues us with tormenting whispers that visit in the quiet of night.

Finding out that our partner was unfaithful is extremely painful. And adding to that pain is the discovery. While some partners may come clean, others get caught, or get caught in the act.

The reasons for straying are not as simple as one might think. Psychologists say, and recent studies show, that double-dipping acts as a temporary fix for a serious problem.

Interestingly, these studies say that the "relationship problem" is the root cause. This means that in many cases both parties share responsibility. There are a myriad of reasons why one might choose door number two, but straying is a band-aid for discourse that does not promote wellness or healing.

I recall my evening with Larry the gemologist. And oh, what a gem. Larry was a creative intellect who thought that online dating was the answer to all of his prayers. After an introductory conversation where he claimed to be an ethical bloke, we met at a classy restaurant overlooking Swan Lake, north of Toronto.

Finally upfront about his escapades, lady lover Larry admitted to having a wife. He confided that he would never pressure Dorothy into "unwanted sex," claiming he loved her too much.

Don't be like Larry.

Till death do us part has a beautiful ring, but sadly, one in two marriages nowadays fail. There are many ways to define a successful relationship, but let's say it means two people who've been together for many years and still care deeply about one another's best interests. It's nasty, but a partner can play foul and love you, all at the same time. No, thank you. We want better.

When a relationship weakens, some will cheat, with devastating results. Why do some Romeos become Pinocchios and some Juliets, Jezebels? There can be many factors at play.

It's common for parties in a relationship to feel unappreciated. This may even occur just as the relationship finds its comfortable groove. This challenge, serious if left unattended, can be met with some tough conversations.

Everyone needs to know that they are valued, loved and desired. A simple chat, a loving act, or a touch of intimacy goes a long way. So folks, set your tables, break out your bagels, and have a vulnerable visit.

"Vulnerability is the birthplace of connection and the path to the feeling of worthiness.

If it doesn't feel vulnerable, the sharing is probably not constructive," says Brené Brown.

When communication flounders, the relationship weakens and opens the door to company. One of the most common reasons for cheating is a lack of communication. Couples who talk have a far greater chance of working through their problems as a team.

Ineffective communication will cause the relationship to falter as each partner struggles alone to solve their problems. In these cases, the relationship may fail. Or those in it, fail to stay faithful.

Infidelity doesn't always occur out of love for another party. It can spring from hate for the current one. Your partner's anger is a formidable foe.

For some, the secrecy factor alone creates a feeling of control over the person they're angry with and seems a fit, fair and final punishment. And an affair can provide both emotional and sexual satisfaction and create a feeling of love and support.

Isolation can make people feel desperate, and desperation makes us behave in ways that are distasteful, even to ourselves. People who stray out of a sense of loneliness experience an awakening. If they've been neglected for a long time, that revitalization feels quite wonderful.

Emotional Intelligence (or EQ, emotional quotient) is the ability to understand and manage our own emotions by reducing stress, communicating effectively, empathizing with others, overcoming challenges, and resolving conflict. A lack of emotional intelligence is a significant contributor to breakdowns that lead to breakups.

Emotional intelligence is a learned skill. However, it's important to understand that there's a difference between learning it and applying it, especially when times are tough. Emotional intelligence is a discipline that takes practice to master. Like exercise. Or giving up cake.

At the end of the day, sometimes love does not conquer all. We may love someone deeply but lose that intimate connection. It just sneaks up on us. We love, but are not in love. When love survives but passion dies, some find fire afar.

Passion is a major factor in the endurance of a relationship. When passion weakens, the relationship changes. In some cases, particularly as we age, physical limitations are a challenge too. But there are things we can do, or do better.

If passion is shaky in your relationship, research "best bedroom behaviour" rather than "sex with strangers."

Boredom may also set in over time and under the sheets. Conversely, when partners are comfortable revealing their erotic fantasies, it leads to exciting new possibilities and pleasures.

A bored partner is easy prey for temptation. Did you know that the very thought of sex releases dopamine in the brain and causes a natural high? Rather than exploring excitement in their own backyard, some seek forbidden fruit elsewhere.

Breaking up is hard for some people to do. So rather than have that anguishing grown-up conversation that ends the relationship, they skip the talk and go straight to bed. The neighbour's bed. And then, they deliberately mess up in a way that makes their cheating easy to discover. This group needs to grow guts.

The good news is that if a couple is genuinely committed to learning from their mistakes, making substantive adjustments and healing, the reward is a shiny new two as one.

It can happen.

CHAPTER TWENTY-FIVE

Surviving Saul

THERE ARE NO UNIVERSAL guidelines regarding infidelity. What is acceptable to some is a betrayal to others. Each relationship must define boundaries that work comfortably with their sensitivity levels and moral compass.

Think about this. While some folks see porn as grand entertainment, others see it as relationship hurt. And while some insist that cheating must be physical, others say that "emotional cheating" is the mother of all fuckups.

What is emotional cheating? This kind of infidelity occurs when one party focuses their time and attention on someone outside the relationship. There is no physical contact, but the investment in another person redirects their energy and focus.

The internet can make it easy to fall from grace. And, like traditional affairs, internet affairs also involve secrecy and lies. An alert and intuitive partner soon senses that something's amiss.

I recognize that there's a rational argument to be made by victims of infidelity, who feel that second chances are imaginary. But not everyone feels that way and not everyone's circumstances accommodate an easy exit.

After first husband Lenny left, I was thirty for a very long year. Until I met Saul.

In order to afford food and rent, I moved into a modest apartment with my two toddlers. My forest green station wagon was fabulous, if not sexy. But it never held me back.

Minutes after moving in, I was in the communal laundry room when a woman with a very thick Israeli accent approached me. Goldie was so friendly that I soon forgot my troubles and focused on hers. Even then, I had a good read on people problems and matters of the heart. But Goldie forgot to mention that the problem was infidelity—hers. She was married to Saul and having an affair with Shlomo the jeweller.

Goldie had a pleasing face and curly blond ringlets. She wore a permanently fake smile and a body that I truly envied. Even with a starvation diet (which meant cutting out cookies), I would never look like Goldie.

That afternoon Goldie invited me for Shabbat dinner. It was a welcome but stunning invite since we had only just met. Goldie told me she was new to Canada, loved cooking and "needed a friend." With enormous chutzpah, or perhaps generosity, she insisted I bring my kids. We each had two toddlers.

Dinner was kind of wonderful. Goldie, her husband Saul and I were all getting along splendidly as broken English merged with bits of Hebrew and dramatic hand gestures. Goldie's husband Saul was a tall, stately man, handsome as hell, with smooth black hair and almond-shaped turquoise eyes. Even with only a smattering of English, he felt like Kansas—a place we call home. A simple man, Saul was sadly lacking in both English and confidence.

The communication was working, the kids were playing, but something about Goldie bothered me. I felt that along with dinner and a smile, she was offering a slice of artificial warmth. Something was off. But dinner was tasty and the kids played well. I love potato kugel and matzo ball soup.

After Shabbat dinner, I never heard from Goldie again, nor did I see her in the building. Perhaps she gave up doing laundry along with returning my calls? But a few weeks after the Shabbat dinner, there was a hard knock on my apartment door. It was Saul. Despite his limited English, I understood he was devastated. So I invited him in for a hot beverage and a cooling off session.

Saul's visits came periodically over the next few months, so I taught him English in order to get the rub (the story, nothing physical). As Saul became more fluent in English, he eventually explained that Goldie had deliberately introduced us at dinner.

Goldie was in love with Shlomo. And, as it turned out, Shlomo had left his wife and was waiting for Goldie at an undisclosed location. It was clear that Goldie had decided in the laundry room that afternoon when she first met me that I would be "good for Saul." Or at least, I could teach him English.

Soon after, Goldie left Saul.

Living in the same apartment building, Saul and I began spending a great deal of time together, entertaining our kids, families and friends. Neither of us could cook, but Saul assured me that if I purchased Israeli food, I would soon become his wife. I love shawarma and hummus—it sounded fair.

So we danced and we ate, and we . . . never mind.

Once again, my home was filled with life, love and laughter. As months turned into years, I fell in love with Saul, the broken cabinetmaker. Although he was not exactly what I had envisioned for my future, we were deeply in love and planned to marry. I had found my happy place.

Until Saul arrived at my door to announce that Goldie had left the country and taken the kids. From Israel, Goldie instructed her son to call his father and threaten that she wouldn't return to Canada until Saul returned to her. (Goldie the manipulator wanted her husband back because her lover, Shlomo, had left her.) But Saul assured me that he would never go back to his "cheating vife."

I trusted him.

When Goldie returned to Canada, Saul seemed confused and unsettled. Our relationship grew tense as I sensed his turmoil. I understood clearly that although Saul wanted to begin a life with me, a life with his children mattered more. Naturally, the children meant everything to him. After months of uncertainty, I received a call that changed the trajectory of my life.

"Feelis, I come over and speak vit you now?" This was unusual. Saul never announced an impending visit.

But I was on my way out for some long-awaited girlfriend therapy and the babysitter was due any minute. "Saul, can we talk on the phone? I'm just on my way out."

"No, I see you. I must see you now."

"Can't it wait until I get back? Please. I'm only going for a few hours."

"Goldie. I slept with Goldie." I heard agony in his voice.

"We are getting back together . . . for the kids . . . only for the kids, Feelis. Only because of the kids. Goldie say if I don't come back to her she will leave again for Israel to live permanently with her sister."

For a few seconds, I thought my mind had melted away or perhaps I had lost my hearing. The confusion didn't last long. I quickly began to feel intense heartache and misery. I felt faint. Saul knew enough English to understand my pain as I moaned softly. It was infidelity, wrapped in loss and hurt.

As his words got through to me, I began to slide down the wall until I was puddled on the bedroom floor screaming, "No!" My voice trailed off as I slumped deeper and deeper into hell.

This can't be happening, I thought.

But it did. I guess Saul said goodbye, but I was lost in grief. And single again.

Thank God for girlfriends.

Months later, I would learn that things didn't work out between Saul and Goldie. Eventually, she returned to Shlomo the jeweller. When Saul called to relate the saga and beg my forgiveness, I told him I wasn't a punching bag. I don't think he ever understood that concept, but he knew it was definitely over.

Infidelity is another word for betrayal. It causes emotional and physical hurt when you discover that someone you love was intimate with another person. It leaves you wracked with grief, your self-esteem plummets and your health suffers, too.

But you will survive.

To be clear, not all affairs are an opportunity for reconciliation. It depends on the parties involved, their ability to look within and their motivation for healing. But when communication is genuine and not focused on blame, survival is possible.

First, the critical and pivotal decision: to end or not to end the relationship? And then the question is how to heal and survive. Or to thrive, despite the infidelity!

Certainly, your happiness, mental health and future are all at risk. And these are decisions that only the two parties involved can make. Supporters and well wishers, please back off. If there is goodness left in the relationship, the parties may be motivated to work through their issues by making significant adjustments. I know several couples who discovered they belonged together after all, reuniting after a second marriage failed.

But let's get real. Cheating is betrayal and betrayal means lying. The offended party has every right to ask for all the answers needed to make an informed decision about moving forward. Transparency is key. Rebuilding trust that's been broken is difficult and may even be impossible. It takes time, patience, and two parties who are committed to rebuilding a solid foundation.

It won't surprise you to learn that although healing is possible, there's no magic elixir. And no one-size-fits-all timetable. This challenge requires significant time and work from both parties.

The word of the day is "motivation."

In any altercation, healing can't occur until the injured party feels heard, understood and validated. Getting real about stuff is tough but having that painful conversation determines if there is any hope for a future. I cannot state this emphatically enough. Only once we learn the root cause of the affair can we make the necessary adjustments to rework, refresh and rekindle a damaged relationship.

So, what should we do when trust is broken?

It's important to put the horse and the cart in the right order. Couples mistakenly think that they must first rebuild trust and then they rebuild the relationship. It doesn't work that way. When trust is broken, it takes a lifetime to rebuild. Sustained transparency is the only behaviour that helps to rebuild trust.

Although it may be frightening and require courage, take a risk. Trust begins by believing that your person is sincere and that their intention to make it work is resolute.

Over time, the infidelity will become a part of your story. Despite the memory that reminds you of a painful time, it will eventually become only a small part of a relationship mosaic that survived a complete meltdown.

I know a loving couple who were high school sweethearts. They separated over an infidelity five years into their marriage. There was a child involved and the injured party's pain was indescribable. She had been drinking, and he had been cheating. Six months later the couple reconciled and she got sober. Today Miriam and Mike are grandparents after 43 years of an exciting and supportive marriage. Now that seems fair.

A word to the transgressor. If you make excuses or blame your partner you can kiss the relationship goodbye. If you've broken trust, your tools are regret and remorse. You must feel remorseful and have the guts to express it. If you do not feel regret, and the remorse is not genuine, then healing is not possible.

As a storyteller, I know how tempting it is to tell tales. Heck, I want to write, post and plaster. Hurt people want to vent and feel validated. But understand that how you feel today may be very different from how you feel tomorrow.

It's also worth noting that wonderful, well-intentioned friends can lessen the chance of romance. When we seek advice from friends, we hear their biases and register their feelings, especially when we're vulnerable and low. And this can muddy the mix.

While it was once shameful to end a marriage, the new shame is staying in a relationship seen as "bad." Sticking with a troubled relationship is considered weakness nowadays. Everyone has an agenda—stick with yours.

If you're committed to making the relationship work, find a therapist who truly cares. There's a damn good chance that tomorrow will be abundantly better than today.

CHAPTER TWENTY-SIX

LGBTQ+ and Jamie

A HEALTHY RELATIONSHIP IS just that, regardless of sexual orientation. My relationship chapters apply universally.

Diverse sexual preferences and gender identity relationships present unique challenges. I learned a lot in my work at Shelley Marshall's Mental Wellness Loft, a public space in Toronto for emotional support, and in the prison system.

Jamie, a British transgender woman, was first detained in a men's prison. After her misfortune, Jamie was moved to Vanier Correctional Centre for Women. And that's where we met.

Jamie was a twenty-five-year old transgender woman, petite and feminine in almost every way. With her flawless fair skin, high cheekbones and shoulder length jet-black bob, she was lovely. But her dark brown eyes had a soulful look that sometimes interrupted what might otherwise appear to be joy.

At first, I thought that Jamie was like any other pretty young lady, but when she and her prison mates explained her plight and preferences, I learned that Jamie had been traumatized in the men's prison. Sadly, and despite her passport identifying her gender as female, she was sent to a men's prison based on her incomplete gender reassignment; Jamie still had a penis.

Gender identities beyond the binary have existed forever. Nevertheless, transgender or gender non-conforming folk are one of the most disadvantaged groups in society. They often endure discrimination, harassment and violence because their gender identity does not correspond with their sex assignment at birth. Whose business is this?

Jamie had come to Canada to find work, make friends and spend romantic time with Lucas, a promising young trans-male. After meeting online, the couple decided to "make things work." They had much in common, and the depth of their understanding for one another was exceptional.

After spending time with a friend in Vancouver, Jamie arrived in Toronto and was detained at Pearson International Airport—and sent to prison. Jamie had overstayed her travel visa in Canada. It was a sad and devastating day.

Not everyone in prison belongs there. And not everyone in segregation is a threat to others. After her experience in the men's prison, Jamie was on suicide watch. We spent many hours in group going over her family life and sexual orientation journey. With compassion for all parties, I learned that Jamie's parents refused to support her in any way.

Jamie could trace her transgender awareness back to her childhood. Even on a good day, "boy" was a bad fit, and for years she never understood why. Sadly, Jamie had spent most of her youth avoiding her gender confusion out of fear, embarrassment and shame.

Psychologists agree that trying to repress one's gender identity never works. In fact, it can be painful and damaging to their emotional and mental wellbeing. As transgender people become more visible in the media and in our communities, it makes it easier for them to feel safer and more comfortable coming out.

Living a truly authentic life is like streaming sunshine.

I am unaware of the legal remedies that eventually freed Jamie. When I visited the segregation unit that week, the ladies reported that Jamie had been unexpectedly released. There was no opportunity to bid her adieu.

In choir fashion they declared, "Jamie's family got involved. She's off to see Lucas!"

We all felt joy that evening (except for the guards, who never understood). I am grateful to Jamie for allowing me into her world in our many Tuesday evening conversations.

Sexuality is complicated. Is it influenced by genes? It's long been a controversial topic.

In a *New York Times* article ("Many Genes Influence Same-Sex Sexuality, Not a Single Gay Gene"), reporter Pam Belluck details an ambitious 2019 genetic study. The analysis of nearly half a million people was the largest ever to analyze the genetics of same sex sexual behaviour. The study found that although genetics play a role, there is no "gay gene."

Researchers found that genetic effects likely account for a third of the influence (about 32 per cent) on whether someone will have same-sex. The remaining contributors included social or environmental factors. Thus, it is impossible for genes to predict sexuality.

We can't pin it on biology, psychology, or life experiences because human sexual attraction is decided by many factors. And there are a myriad of ways in which human sexuality manifests itself—the variations are endless.

How about we just advocate for understanding and tolerance?

Healthy relationships differ, but all should exhibit care and concern for the parties involved. Some healthy LGBTQ+ relationships, like some straight relationships, include consensual non-monogamous arrangements. This may include three or more parties, all thriving beautifully, with or without children. In fact, healthy LGBTQ+ relationships are characterized by resilience, creativity and uniqueness.

The world can be so hostile. It is critical that LGBTQ+ relationships provide a safe landing where everyone feels free. Healthy liaison partners respect one another's chosen gender pronouns, chosen names and personal boundaries. They allow time for personal interests and never threaten to out you. Most importantly, no one must ever be forced to have sex in a way that is either emotionally or physically uncomfortable.

Abusers may claim that disrespectful or violent behaviour in an LGBTQ+ relationship is normal, but that is simply untrue. Lesbian, gay, bisexual, transgender, questioning and queer people have healthy relationships just like heterosexual folks.

If you are LGBTQ+, you can face unique obstacles in seeking help, most notably when you are first coming out. Know that you are not alone, and there are places specifically designed to assist you in both your transition and your relationships.

As an advocate for diversity, I feel that everyone is entitled to kindness and respect. I pray that inclusivity becomes the societal norm, and that collectively we accept everyone without the need to question or condemn.

CHAPTER TWENTY-SEVEN

My fiancé

I WAS MARRIED TWICE: once too young, and once too tired. But in between marriages, there was a quick engagement. Or what some may call "a little something something" to tide me over.

Years after my first marriage ended, having exhausted the boys, the men and the synagogue singles, I joined Sabra International. Sabra was a dating service for the over-thirty, fabulously flirty Jewish population. But my high-speed road to happiness turned out to be a descent into hell.

Sabra upheld their end of the mating bargain. They fixed me up with a few good men, all of whom were Jewish—all of whom I swiftly rejected, except one. I had been betting that Prince Charming would present the glass slipper. And he did.

He was a handsome man. Paul was tall, thinly built and sharply dressed. He had a closely-trimmed black beard, a broad smile and perfect teeth. Sexy and masculine. He was highly intelligent, an interesting storyteller and outrageously funny. We laughed until the end and then we cried.

When we began to date, it was romantic anticipation and unbridled passion. Paul was a television extra and a talented portrait artist. As such, he paid attention to my hair, makeup, wardrobe and even how I spoke. I must admit that the admiration was addictive. I couldn't wait to see him and the time between our dates was always too long.

Paul was full of surprises. One evening he invited over a few of our closest friends to unveil a stunning portrait that he had recently created. It was a painting of me and my son Michael at Michael's Bar Mitzvah. That evening, I took the portrait home, perched it against the wall and thought: Girlfriend, you just couldn't be happier.

But a week later, I entered my apartment to discover evidence of a savage break-in. My suite was stripped to the walls, except for the portrait. They had even ripped up the broadloom in a quest for buried treasures, and although I had none, the violation felt disgusting and creepy.

So what does a woman do when she's confused and hysterical?

I called Paul. An hour later, he arrived at my door with comfort and a surprise in a small box. So, with a generous, gorgeous marquise cut diamond, we became formally engaged. Surprise number two!

We did not set a wedding date. Although Paul was anxious to wed, I had a strange, nagging doubt. At the time, I was in my late thirties and I was receiving a do-not-marry signal from an unknown source. A bizarre feeling when you think you're in love.

Nevertheless, soon after becoming engaged we bought a home together. It was a lovely wartime bungalow on a quiet street, with a library on one side and a subway on the other. We fixed it up like a dollhouse and were blissful. Until a few years into the dollhouse when Paul awoke one morning with startling news: surprise number three.

"I have something to tell you," he said softly.

Odd, I thought, first thing in the morning.

"What's up?" I asked, thinking it was a problem with his son or a fight with his mom.

"I have AIDS, and I'm gay," he announced calmly, seeming almost proud.

I jumped out of bed and pivoted to face him. "What?!"

"I think you heard me," he responded with a finality like there was nothing more to discuss.

"That's it? That's all? How do you know? How . . ." I trailed off, feeling my energy drain.

So many questions that would never be answered.

"A few years ago, I was a bit . . . ah . . . promiscuous. You know, kinda playful with guys. I was fearful for a while that I might have AIDS, but when nothing materialized, I just put it behind me and carried on."

"No!" I screamed, interrupting his meagre explanation. "You carried on? You carried on with me! You had a test when we met—a negative test. Did you lie? Otherwise, why would you think you have AIDS now?"

Realizing my lethal exposure, I was frightened into madness as thoughts raced through my mind, mostly about my kids. I feared for my life and was mentally planning their care.

"I have shingles. It's often the first sign of HIV," came his casual response.

"Have you been tested?"

"No. I just know," said the resigned whisper of a man who had done his homework.

At age forty, Paul thought he had beaten the system by outliving his best before date. He explained that he wasn't fussy about who he had sex with—both men and women were great. But, on second thought, he might actually prefer men.

Following a bizarre discussion, it was decided that Paul would move into the guest room and we would repeat our AIDS tests. Mine came back negative and his was, indeed, positive. That meant that either Paul had lied about his negative test when we met, or he had been promiscuous while we were together.

It didn't matter.

We live and we learn, don't we? I learned that a person is more likely to develop shingles if their immune system is compromised, and that includes people with untreated or advanced HIV.

The engagement ended and we sold the little house on Park Home Avenue. Paul moved in with his mother who was horribly domineering and filthy rich. And I began a series of tests.

The AIDS epidemic was scary and overwhelming. The world watched in shock as healthy young men became ill and died. Scientists had few answers for the many questions that people had about this horrifying illness. Perhaps most disturbing, the disease primarily affected groups that were misrepresented and misunderstood. So for years, authorities largely turned their backs on the growing epidemic.

In 1991, the Red Ribbon Project was launched to create a symbol of compassion and awareness for people living with AIDS and their caregivers. Still, little was known about the illness other than the means of transmission, its horrible symptoms and that a positive diagnosis usually led to death. Antiviral drugs coming on the market seemed to only briefly prolong life.

For me, the testing process was a terrifying and deeply humiliating nightmare. It was one fearful test after the other. At the time, periodic tests were required. With each test, I prayed.

I knew fear, I knew secrecy and I knew shame.

I sent my kids to live with their dad and indulged in a six-month meltdown. I stopped mothering, stopped socializing and gave up on life. In spite of my paranoia, test after test was signalling survival. I had surprised an entire city of immunologists. One day a doctor with frazzled hair like Einstein announced, "By all accounts, Phyllis Taylor, you should be dead."

And the next specialist jokingly said, "Most likely you're just a wee ghost."

Nothing cheered me up.

Except my brother, Allan. Well into this ordeal, he had made a career change. Instead of selling stereo equipment, Al was now selling life insurance. Unannounced, he arrived on my doorstep one day with his lovely wife, Jan, and a desire to end my misery. He was about to request a life insurance quality AIDS test.

After weeks of agony awaiting results, I will never forget his findings.

"Phyllis," he said sternly. And then slowly proclaimed, "We invest in life. Our test is golden . . . you don't have HIV."

After Allan's endorsement, I engineered an appointment with the top AIDS specialist in Toronto, and, once again, tested negative. Even Dr. Special was shocked. He explained that much was still unknown, but it was believed that a few individuals were immune to the virus. (We now know that just under ten per cent of people are born with some form of natural immunity to HIV.) He said that I had a genetic mutation (of course, we always knew I had some mutation), and it was this that saved my life.

A year later Paul died. There, but for the grace of genes, go I.

The universe had blessed me lavishly. I promised to give back. Twenty years later the prison doors opened, and I was able to satisfy my vow.

CHAPTER TWENTY-EIGHT

Clusterfucks!

IN A WOMEN'S PRISON, same-sex frolics are a way of life, and group sex is a common sport. You could even say it replaces yoga. While many inmates keep it hidden, others discuss their sexual stretches and never feel a blush. And then there are women whose bedroom behaviour was a career that earned them a prison stay. Prostitution.

This story takes place in the general population of a Canadian prison for women.

Women inmates come from diverse cultural backgrounds, different economic classes and all education levels. There are highly educated gals and others with only street smarts.

There are rich women, poor women, married women, single woman and pregnant women who risk a cell birth without the help of a doula. The more fortunate ladies in labour are handcuffed, carted out of corrections and marched through hospitals in a humiliating walk of pain.

Just like us, prisoners hunger for respect, support and understanding. They share a need to belong.

I was delivering a lesson series, Psychology of Friendship when, two weeks in, a woman pleaded for privacy. After class, Brandy confided that she and two others had formed a triangle of tenderness—a lesbian arrangement. In a women's prison, the girls can't be fussy about gender.

All three women were incredibly beautiful and earned their living as working girls on a street corner in downtown Toronto. Let's just say they were business acquaintances. Outside the prison they competed for business. Inside, they competed for each other's affection.

The three ladies were apprehended and escorted to prison within weeks of one another. News travels quickly, especially when sex is involved. And so, as each of the ladies was admitted to prison, they quickly found each other. It would have been fine, perhaps even fun, if they had just remained pals. But instead, two fell in love with the third and formed a triangular tryst.

Prison relationships are an interesting study. There is extreme love and extreme hate, with little neutrality. And normative behaviour is at a premium. Despite the easy exchange of love partners, however, not everyone has a vibrant sex life. In fact, many prefer conversation over fornication.

Brandy was a beautiful, tall, full-figured thirty-year-old Brazilian babe with long, blond, wavy hair who bragged that she had never known any other source of income. She claimed she was the best in the business. Brandy specialized in women, but boasted a large client roster split evenly between the sexes.

When Brandy was ten, her mom went to prison for chopping up Billy the butcher. (Billy had been a bad beau.) Brandy was raised by her Aunt Francesca. Auntie, who was forever forty and finally single, explained to Brandy that while she liked marriage, she preferred entertaining for money. Francesca taught Brandy to love men and make money.

With a big personality to match her stature, Brandy had a loud voice and hysterical giggle. As an imaginative and colourful storyteller, as Brandy told things, life was good.

When Brandy returned to the women's prison for her third term, she quickly resumed her role as Top Dog, both honoured and feared. Top Dog is a title reserved for an established cell warrior who, with a crew of trusted followers, assists inmates by garnering friendly affection in exchange for defending their prison spats.

Ruby was a petite Irish redhead with lots of hair and mounds of curls. When Ruby put her hair up in bobby pins, she looked like a ballroom dancer. Over forty and under five feet tall, Ruby was quiet and seldom smiled. When she did speak, her sweet Irish accent coloured a story of sadness, isolation and sexual abuse.

Ruby had suffered at the hands of a physical abuser back home. Before coming to Canada at the age of sixteen, Ruby had been raised by an alcoholic stepdad who thought that Ruby was both his housemaid and punching bag. While Ruby was making meals and sorting laundry, step daddy was drinking up money and planning his next heist. Ruby's face was flawless, but her childhood had left her with deep emotional scars.

What seemed to keep Ruby afloat was her proud portfolio. She boasted of being the best oral provider on planet sex—and said it like she'd won a Nobel Prize. This was Ruby's first time in prison, and she swore she'd never be back. She was not overly fond of the bed.

Raven was shockingly beautiful with ice blue eyes, puffy lips and striking black hair. It was "Elvis black" with that stunning hint of blue. Raven carried herself like a runway model. She was intelligent and well-spoken; extraordinarily sophisticated. But her air of confidence leaned towards an arrogance seldom seen in prison.

Born in Texas, Raven had migrated to Canada five years earlier looking for a hot guy and a cool job. Finding neither, Raven took to the streets. At thirty-five, she was still looking for her soulmate and hadn't yet ruled out children.

One day, Raven shared her prison sentiments with me.

"I cannot overstate how degrading the prison experiment is. Every time we receive a visitor, go to court or attend a medical appointment we're stripped down in front of two guards and told to bend over, squat, and cough. The assumption is that we're always concealing drugs."

"Wouldn't that make you want to avoid the doctor?"

"It's the most degrading experience imaginable. Women who've been raped or violated in the past are triggered and inconsolable. What they're doing here is re-traumatizing anyone who's experienced sexual assault."

"You get so accustomed to the loss of dignity in prison that hope melts into hopelessness."

And I said, "Can we work on a career change, Raven?"

Raven just smiled that day, but months later took me up on the offer. She's rumoured to be modelling part-time now. And the other part we're just not sure.

I learned that Brandy, Ruby and Raven were not their real names, but I never found out how they ended up on the same cell block. Not surprisingly though, after the trio scored the same digs, the jailhouse began to rock. But as their friendship deepened, jealously raised its ugly head. Their alliance was inevitable and so were their problems.

The inmates loved Brandy, Ruby and Raven. In fact, many women were inspired by them and sought to join their circle. In prison, it passes the time nicely when you've got good pals. So, these ladies generously shared their stories and entertained the crowd.

The problems began when Brandy, Ruby and Raven became so damn friendly they began sampling each other's talents. And since ladies can't cozy in lockup, they make up for it in the shower.

There's not much privacy in a prison shower. A dozen or so shower heads are affixed to the walls, and flimsy shower curtains allow for easy access. The ladies say that guards are actually aware of shower sex but seem not to mind. And so, Brandy, Ruby, and Raven would shower together, save water and share love.

It was all quite civil, actually, until Raven fell in love with Brandy. And Ruby did too. While Brandy enjoyed an exuberance of love, Raven and Ruby were constantly duelling for affection. And the contest was raw.

The ladies sought my guidance. I was deeply troubled and urged them to approach their caseworkers. There was little I could do to stop the insanity and prayed for a cooling off period. I counselled them each separately and spoke with them collectively. I explained that they had gone down a dangerous path and begged them to stop. I made it clear that a relationship triangle may feel like a world of love, but it could easily result in pain.

There was constant drama and tears. As Raven and Ruby competed for Brandy's affection, something was about to blow. A prison quickie may sound like a great mood stabilizer, but a healthy emotional bond is inconceivable. In prison, love is more likely to detonate and when that happens, inmates are transferred to disciplinary segregation.

That's exactly what happened. I arrived at the prison one afternoon to whispers that all three ladies were off the unit. Their colleagues reported that they had been "thrown in seg" until further notice.

One guard, entertained by the breaking news, described the saloon-style brawl.

"Animal Kingdom, today, Phyllis, luckily there were no weapons. But I mean they had a hair-pulling, kicking and screaming round of combat on the dining room floor at breakie."

"Raven scratched Ruby's face, Ruby destroyed Raven's uniform, and they both lay crying in the fetal position until we carted them off. Brandy was cool eh, but they're all in lockup now," said Charlie, a rather funny English officer with a quirky hint of humanity.

Following solitary confinement, all three women would be assigned to separate units, never to ignite again.

When Brandy returned to class a week later, she was the effervescent gal we all adored. Throughout the entanglement, I had sensed that Brandy was in it for fun, or perhaps exercise. She was never emotionally invested. Given the opportunity, Brandy would indulge again.

It was different for Raven and Ruby. Both of them loved Brandy deeply and were badly hurt. These ladies had experienced severe emotional pain, and the healing process was overwhelming. My heart ached for them.

After the breakup, it took several months until things returned to normal. In life, we learn from everyone on our path. I continue to ask myself if I should have done more to protect the ladies. I see my role in prison as fixing the broken pieces. But some women don't feel they're worth fixing.

When we think of romantic relationships, many of us still think of Love Story or Pretty Woman. These are movie tales where a man and a woman meet, fall wildly in love and are committed "till death do us part." That is monogamy.

Some call it plain vanilla.

In today's society, there's a growing interest in exploring something different. Some people want to expand their romantic objectives to include others. I call it alternate arrangements.

Polyamory is the act of having an intimate relationship with more than one person at the same time. This is not to be confused with polygamy, which involves being married to multiple partners. Polygamy is illegal in North America, although in 2020 Utah passed a law to decriminalize polygamy, reducing bigamy among consenting adults from a third-degree felony punishable by prison time, to an infraction on par with a speeding ticket as reported by Ben Winslow, Fox 13 News Utah.

We know that identification and gender preferences are inherent, experientially influenced and socially powered. Polyamory is more elusive. Some people suggest that they're born polyamorous, while others argue that wanting a poly relationship is a decision, not a condition.

An open relationship refers to any intimate or sexual relationship that is consensually non-monogamous—a couple who agree to have sex with others. This may occur as the couple is forming their relationship or later. They may form an established threesome or welcome newcomers, temporarily or permanently. And while some couples find "company" a vacation treat, others make it a year round sport.

The most important characteristic of polyamory is the knowledge and consent of all parties. That's fair, right?

Take "swingers" for example. These folks are in a committed relationship, but engaging in recreational sex with people they may or may not know. It's like one would casually change dance partners out on the ballroom floor.

One problem with open relationships is jealousy, just as we saw in our prison cluster. Jealousy is deeply rooted in the human psyche. It wreaks havoc.

I saw another example of the pain polyamory can cause while dating a few years back. On our first date, Bruce, then in his late fifties, sensed compassion and shared his story. He was a family lawyer and photo hobbyist. His marriage to Joyce was, by mutual agreement, "open." A year into this blissful arrangement, it fell apart for Bruce.

Joyce decided she no longer loved him and was off to start a new life with Jerry, her lover. In her exuberance to begin anew in New York, Joyce had turned both of the children against Bruce. Alone and lonely, he was in crisis and seriously suicidal.

Many couples who agree to try polyamory may do so as a sort of adhesive. And that says something. The relationship was coming unglued before the decision was made to expand the partner roster. While engaging in polyamory might seem like a fun fix, seek counselling instead.

Polyamory is a controversial lifestyle and, from my perspective, only works in unique circumstances. The deck is stacked against this arrangement. When one party finds someone they connect with on an intensely intimate and emotional level, the novelty wins and the original relationship loses. And, sadly, children may be caught in the crosshairs.

CHAPTER TWENTY-NINE

Know when to fold 'em

"HOW WILL I KNOW when to leave?"

If your feelings and needs are unmet, if you express concern and encounter insults, insinuations, and criticism, or if you stop sharing your stuff altogether—you are in trouble. If your joy is irrelevant to Prince Charming (or Sleeping Beauty), it's time for a change.

The term "trauma bonding" describes an emotional attachment, otherwise known as Stockholm syndrome. In these situations, loyalty develops between a victim and their abuser. While Stockholm situations are rare, loyal abuse victims are not.

Despite their fear and suffering, victims are often confused and this is especially true when bad behaviour is punctuated with random acts of kindness and intimacy.

Many say it's not possible to love an abuser. Our minds are hardwired to move toward ecstasy and away from agony. Fear and love are opposite emotional states, and cannot coexist. Tainted by fear, love becomes something else.

Abuse is used to gain and maintain power and control. Come to think of it, outside of romantic relationships, abuse is simply called bullying.

Abuse varies, severity fluctuates and all of it is unpredictable. And different forms of abuse overlap and intersect in the same ugly arena.

After my first marriage ended, I decided to lose weight and gain a lover, but it turned out to be a lot more complicated. About three months into my separation, I was invited to attend a neighbourhood watch party. The event was dubbed Singles Watching Singles, and each person was to wear a toy watch. My cousin Ruth invited me, but a headache had kept her at home. So gutsy and determined to begin a new chapter, I set out to round up a beau.

It was a silly event that would have dampened my dating spirits had it not been for Rob. I was headed home when Rob called me back from the door. We had not been introduced, but he read my name tag and made a bold move. Such chutzpah!

"May I have your number?" he asked with a charming smile.

I was so impressed with his gallantry that I shouted my number back before fleeing the noisy gathering. A day later, Rob called. With his ultra-soft voice, Rob asked me to join him for a cup of tea and slice of lemon pie.

"Rob, I'm newly separated, haven't dated in years."

"What could it hurt?" he asked with a Jewish inflection that revealed some character and a hint of humour.

"Okay," I said, "But KISS . . . Keep It Simple, Sexy."

There was no response.

Those first post-marital dates can be so awkward, but it helped that Rob was handsome. With a tall, thick build, reddish hair cropped military style, golden brown eyes and a welcoming smile, I thought he might just do the trick.

It really didn't take much. Before I knew it, we were a thing. Rob seemed special, but he had very muted emotional responses. Still, he was so patient with my kids that he might have been auditioning for daddy of the year. Rob revealed that he had secretly resolved that I would be his first wife. How flattering. Rob's accommodating nature and unwavering support might have made him a contender.

But my little inner voice said big things: "nisht far mir" (not for me). Being an exuberant, sociable soul, I was unfamiliar with passive. Rob's relaxed nature left me fluctuating between wonderment, disappointment, and boredom.

A few months into our relationship, I decided that stock trader Rob did not pass the cognitive ability test. He could not solve problems, make decisions or use language to communicate intelligently. Rob wasn't just passive, he was surprisingly simple.

I also uncovered a big lie. Rob had added eight years to his age to appear to be a more capable "daddy"—although my kids' birth father already played an active and loving role. Worse yet was his under achieving performance under the covers. I was thirty-one and it would be my first time ending a relationship. This should be fun.

As Rob arrived for our regular date, I requested a kitchen chair chat. Agreeable as always, Rob sat across from me at the table. Calmly and with much respect, I explained to Rob that we were not a great match. Okay, I might also have mentioned that he was a bit simple and that we should stop seeing one another immediately.

Following my brief speech, Rob silently glared at me. His eyes began to widen, then darken. The tension mounted in silence. I was becoming unnerved and frightened. Before I could fully register his sudden mood change, Rob bounded from his chair and began violently smashing me against the kitchen counter. As I was screaming "stop!" he was screaming profanities. After beating me, Rob fled the house. I was left motionless on the floor, weak and in shock.

Thank God the kids were upstairs with a loving nanny and a loud cartoon.

Most abusive relationships don't start out with a swollen lip. No, they begin like any other love with just enough wonderful to proceed. But in abusive relationships, before you know it, you're groomed and ready to accept blame for things beyond your control. Slowly, or perhaps not so slowly, love on a sandy beach evolves into love on the rocks.

Having seen no earlier signs of abuse, I was stunned. Pain and humiliation were competing for my attention. With caution, I crawled across the floor. The phone was affixed to the wall. Feeling ashamed and in severe pain, I pulled myself up and called Lenny. Yes, ex-husband Lenny.

Minutes later, Lenny arrived in a rusty old Cutlass Supreme with his shiny new fiancée. Despite my humiliation, Lenny made light of my situation and escorted me to the emergency department. The police were called.

As we've seen before (the case of inmate Trish for example), an abused party does not press charges. A victim of domestic abuse can make a complaint, but it's the police who decide whether to lay charges. In general, the police are directed by law to lay charges where there are probable grounds that an illegal offence was committed.

The police charged Rob with domestic violence, and he immediately began terrorizing my home and workplace. He stole my car, made incessant crank calls and hid in the shadows outside my house. Thank God for good neighbours—they reported him twice.

A month later, my wounds were healing, but my life was a nightmare. With the help of my lawyer (also my friend and employer), we urged the police to drop charges. (Sometimes these deviant offenders continue hitting back until we back off.) As soon as the charges were dropped, the stalking did too.

Here's to short relationships and lasting intuition!

How does one endure abuse from a lover, when love means protect? For me, abuse was limited to a single episode of violence and an evening stalker. Every abuse dilemma is unique and complicated. But we are all better off without the looming fear of abuse. Personal safety and a wonderful life are our best revenge.

There will be times when escaping an abusive relationship doesn't seem possible. But there are always options, my friends.

How do you recognize abuse? Physical abuse may include punching, hitting, slapping, kicking, strangling or physically restraining a partner against their will. It may also include reckless driving, or making someone's physical space feel unsafe.

Sexual abuse may involve rape or any forced sexual act. It can also be withholding sex or using it as a weapon. An abusive partner might also use sex to criticize or demean their partner.

It's important to note that marital rape is a real thing. Spousal rape is the act of sexual intercourse without consent. The act need not involve physical violence. Marital rape is a form of both domestic violence and sexual abuse, but proving spousal rape is often difficult. Although lack of consent is easily proven in cases involving strangers, spouses who would normally have consensual sex must prove resistance.

Emotional abuse can be just as devastating as physical abuse and involves fear, guilt and shame. These abusers engage in behaviour that insults, threatens, rejects, neglects, blames, manipulates, isolates, degrades, punishes, humiliates or exerts control. The feelings associated with emotional abuse are confusing and leave the victim to sort fact from fiction. Because the abuser's words and behaviour are often perplexing, it is difficult to decode or describe.

In discussing abuse one afternoon, an inmate told me, "I didn't think I was being abused. I had begun to believe Ben's lies. He made me feel stupid and ugly. He even had me believing that no one else wanted me. Years later, when I began to confide in my sister, I realized that his behaviour was cruel and abusive."

This inmate was so intimidated by her abusive partner that she was afraid to say "no." When he asked her to sell drugs on his behalf, she did. During the second sale, Sylvia was caught. Sent to prison, she had nowhere to turn. Boyfriend had taken off with a new sweetie.

Emotional abusers have mastered the skill. Their victims spend countless hours trying to figure out what triggers the abuser's repulsive behaviour and then change their own in an effort to escape their wrath.

Psychological abuse occurs when one partner, through language and behaviour, wears away at the other's mental wellbeing and makes them doubt their sanity. This crazy-making is also known as "gaslighting," after the 1938 British stage play, *Gas Light*. The play features a nasty manipulative husband who tries to slowly drive his wife mad.

Financial abuse is also common. Keep in mind that abuse is about power and control. The financial abuser may not allow their partner to earn money, control the bank accounts, seek credit, or run up debts.

Cultural abuse occurs when a victim's cultural identity is used to inflict suffering or gain control. Refusing to let someone observe the dietary or dress customs of their faith, using racial slurs, threatening to out someone as LGBTQ+, or isolating someone who doesn't speak the local language are examples of cultural abuse.

People everywhere are dealing with violence and abuse. No one has the right to hurt you or your children. Help is a phone call away: in Canada and the US, text HOME to 741741 to connect with a Crisis Counsellor. The Crisis Text Line serves anyone in crisis, providing free, 24/7 support via text messaging.

Living with abuse is unacceptable, unfixable and non-negotiable. But there are other, fuzzier, relationship challenges that are harder to label.

Addiction is another serious challenge. Substance abuse (alcohol, drugs, etc.) or behavioural abuse (gambling, rape, etc.) have consistently damaging and escalating effects on the relationship. In a decade spent with prisoners who struggle with substance or behavioural addiction, I have seen the devastating results.

For starters, it is impossible to trust a using addict. Cravings force addicts to lie to get their next fix. They need their drug ready for the coming dreaded withdrawal. All of today's activities focus on tomorrow's fix. An addict is concerned more with their needs than those of their partner or children. A loving partner is left with feelings of anger and betrayal.

Some addictions are treatable. With proper intervention and care, the damage can be repaired, and a couple may experience healing. Because the viability of each relationship must be considered on its own merits, a counsellor can recommend whether rebuilding the relationship is viable or if ending it is preferable.

There are still other signals that urge "fold 'em." While every relationship experiences bumps that cause couple connections to fray, there are cases when every channel of communication is blocked. Your partner has left the building. This is emotional abandonment, and a strong signal that you might want to reconsider your own commitment.

And then there are narcissists. Anyone can be a little self-serving from time to time in an effort to survive and thrive, but narcissism is another matter. According to a medical professional review performed by the Cleveland Clinic, experts estimate that up to 5 per cent of our population has narcissistic personality disorder, explaining that NPD is one of ten personality disorders. These disorders cause those affected to think, feel and act out in ways that hurt themselves—and of course others.

But understand that a narcissist does not have to be a full-scale creep to wreak havoc. Depending upon where your narcissist registers on the spectrum, life can be brutal. There's no sugar coating it. Being in a relationship with a narcissist is like a severe electric shock; it leaves you limp. Narcissists are focused on themselves, need constant attention, and go ballistic over mild criticism. They think they're never wrong and they excel at everything.

The traits of narcissistic personality disorder include:

Lack of empathy	Depends on admiration	Over-active aggression
Controlling	Must have needs met	Sense of entitlement
Manipulative	Cares not for needs of others	Won't accept criticism

Sense of superiority

These puppies do not make great lovers or love interests.

Leaving a relationship is never easy, but if you've been emotionally abandoned or struck with a narcissist, you might not be sorry. Having been a single parent myself, I urge couples to do everything in order to make it work. And then try harder. However, if every reasonable avenue has been explored, and life is but a bitch, chances are the kids hurt, too. It's time to move on.

Living in the past, when it used to be wonderful, or in the future, where it's "gonna get good," is false hope. For optimum emotional health, one must live in the moment. The connection between mind and body is powerful. If we disregard messages of the mind today, our bodies won't thank us tomorrow.

CHAPTER THIRTY

That's what friends are for

AH FRIENDSHIP, thou art my elixir.

Not all relationships are about romantic love. Some of the deepest feelings we have are for people we call friends.

Let's get something straight: there's a difference between men and women. Men derive more emotional support and therapeutic value from their intimate partners than from their friendships. With friends, men tend to talk facts in a sporty, activity-based setting. Female friends, by contrast, share intimate, relational and reactional issues.

Here's another shocker. Women are typically more demanding when it comes to friendship and seek a stronger emotional attachment. We require more special time with our friends, while men are generally content coasting on casual.

While some folks do well alone, most of us crave company. I am a people junkie. For me, friendship and breathing compete for first place. But not every friendship is a gift. My friend Monique's mom said it best: "Real friends are like taxis on a rainy day. You're lucky to find one."

Since belonging and intimacy are essential, living in isolation causes a significant level of depression and emotional suffering. The antidote for loneliness is experiencing connection. Intimacy, and only intimacy, will provide the satisfaction of belonging and closeness.

On darker days, the presence of an understanding, supportive and loyal friend is a game changer. Often, it's our friends who affect a meaningful shift or steer us away from disaster.

But friendship is an interesting kind of love, isn't it? There is no contract, no promise of love, no specific rules of engagement. But there are some "friend essentials."

Trust. Our confidences are kept eternally. Even when we clash and dash, this friend doesn't spill our beans. It isn't just the strength of the friendship, but our friend's ethical code that determines the safety of secrets.

Authenticity. If friends ask for an opinion or guidance, they are counting on honest feedback. Speaking falsely to make someone feel good is detrimental to their realization and decision making. Even friends with low intuition will sense falseness. Truthful and straightforward responses build trust. Words matter.

Respect. A simple concept: we give it, we get it. Everyone deserves respect. Indeed, we teach others how to treat us. Too often I've heard people put themselves down and then wonder why others think less of them.

Forgiving. A friendship can't survive when one is stuck on yesterday's flaws—fast forward. Along with forgiveness, there's understanding and compassion. Ultimately, a friend forgives a bad when it's followed with sincere remorse and an earnest demonstration (not just talk) of doing better.

Support. Being there for you is a pleasure not a punishment. Supportive friends will help us examine the advantages of transforming a shaky life, or remodelling the kitchen. While they may disagree with our choices, the support is solid. These friends are genuine and have no personal agenda.

For me, public speaking means synagogue gigs and community gangs. Several sincere dear friends frequently show up to support me. Surrounded by love, it feels like my own Bat Mitzvah!

Empathy. There are three components to empathy: cognitive, emotional and compassionate. Compassionate empathy is a concern for or ability to grasp someone else's life, and then relate, comfort and, if appropriate, provide gentle guidance.

Dependability. Dependability is showing up—on time. And focusing on the friendship rather than the cellphone. If you don't honour today, I won't count on you for tomorrow. Those who falter lose credibility, reliability, and integrity. If the offence is repeated enough, disappointed friends may wander yonder.

Thoughtful. Visits are still in vogue! Visiting a friend who is shut-in is a memorable and valuable gift (call first). Bring a coffee or bring a treat. Actually, nothing says loving like an oversized cranberry bran muffin.

Listening. I'm a born communicator. I engage and encourage others to speak their truth. But I'm still on the learning curve for listening skills.

By listening not only for the facts but also for the feelings, I learn that we are all in struggle or following a dream—often at the same time. I have long felt that a dash of kindness and a sprinkle of compassion mix incredibly well.

Listen to show support, validate to invoke confidence, and for God's sake, let everyone know that they're not alone. It's an honour to walk beside a friend, to guide them or to simply hold their hand.

We must all have a dream: a purpose or a passion. Listening is an opportunity to help a friend close the gap between where they sit and where they must stand. With a profound understanding of what is being shared, we encourage positive actionable behaviour: a simple step that will bring one closer to a goal.

Lately, I've met some profoundly wonderful women. When meeting someone new, I listen to discover as much about them as they're comfortable sharing. Mostly about their life and journey.

I'm interested in the qualities that point to integrity and matters of the heart. I silently observe their interaction with others and seek an understanding of who they are and how they arrived.

And I listen to "see" if they too are listening to me.

Humour. With laughter, worry disappears—a transition into utopia. Laughter, however brief, is a stress reliever, an entertainment and a bonding mechanism. Laughter hooks us into coming back. When I ask men and women about the qualities they like in a friend, humour is high on the list.

At times we need a friend, and at other times, we must be one.

Club memberships offer additional benefits. I am a volunteer enthusiast and enjoy being of service. My empathy and strong emotional connections are invaluable as a life coach and motivational speaker. The ability to build trust and encourage people to share their story is a reliable channel for bonding.

As president of my Hadassah and B'nai Brith chapters, I was actively involved in fundraising and equally involved in friend-making. Volunteer positions present unique opportunities to make friends and form bonds. If you're a wallflower, you may dream about people approaching you, but it doesn't work that way. Stretch beyond your comfort zone and approach the friendliest folk in the room.

We are not born with beliefs. Every belief, including those about ourselves, is learned through personal experience and messaging from others. A belief that something is possible encourages positive action. Often our belief system is informed by the encouragement and enthusiasm of friends who believe in us—it makes a difference.

Friends take pride in our achievements. If your friend is not applauding your success, it's the bright green kiss of jealousy. "Compersion," the antithesis of jealousy, is the happiness and joy experienced by others when we have an uplifting experience. In Yiddish, we call this kvelling (bursting with pride).

If you can't partake in my joy, you can't partake in my life.

Emotions are contagious. Our spirit is affected by people who are afraid, anxious, or helpless. Why do we experience emotion while watching The Young and the Restless? The words, actions and facial expressions of the actors change our emotional state. This happens in real life too.

So what about rejection? We live in a world where judging others is a conversation starter. Or a conversation ender. I still remember an incident from ten years ago at a coffee shop gathering organized by B'nai Brith. After a lifelong battle with the bathroom scale, I had just begun the healthy girl plan, so I ordered a coffee and passed on my official donut.

I was quietly seated at the roundtable, when zaftig (plump) Zella plopped herself down and shouted, "No donuts tonight, Phyllis?"

"Not tonight, Zella," I smiled proudly. "Just started a plan!"

"Ya, 'til the next time," she said throwing her head back in uncontrollable laughter as she looked to others for support. No one raised their head.

"Next time. Next time what?" I pressed, annoyed as hell.

Looking awkward, Zella laughed and muttered, "The next time someone puts a donut near you. That'll do it."

Expressionless, I picked up my coffee and moved to another table.

Laughter does not make Foul Fanny funny.

I never forgot Zella and her crappy public shaming. From that day on, each time I thought junk food, I thought Zella, and turned off the junk switch. Today, when I teach addiction management, I share my story and ask everyone to dig up a Zella.

Integrity inspires us to be more accepting and less judgmental. When I struggle with judgment, I think of Hyla Saunders.

Hyla, thank you for never judging me. You don't judge me when I tell you something I'm not proud of, when I take a chance on a dating site, or when I eat cake. You're an exceptional person and a valued friend. It's an amazing feeling to know, that when I walk with you, I walk in a judgement-free zone.

Not all friendships are created normally. I remember attending Vanier Correctional during the holiday season when the women were aglow with festive spirit. Christmas in prison is not a gift and many suffer serious episodes of depression. But today was somehow different, and the women were buzzing with enthusiasm.

When I asked what the deal was, Carla said, "Follow us!"

Volunteers are instructed not to enter the cell block (sleeping quarters) unless escorted by a guard. There wasn't one in sight, so in the spirit of Christmas kindness I followed the women to their quarters.

Arriving at Cell Block "C," I understood homemade glee. Prison management was running a unit decorating contest for the holidays and the ladies were in prize pursuit. Apparently, they had teamed up on the cell decor.

Carla said, "We referred to your Team Building booklet."

A profound feeling of pleasure and fulfillment washed over me. A dozen of the most resourceful gals had utilized every scrap of tin foil, toilet paper, tampons and an assortment of hygiene and dietary products to adorn their space. The flowers were spectacular. The creativity that I witnessed that day would make Picasso smile. And the bonds of friendship were irresistible to see.

For me, the encouragement of friends has made all the difference.

It was the encouragement of friends that convinced me to write this book.

CHAPTER THIRTY-ONE

The heartbreak of over

W HEN WEIGHTY ISSUES OCCUR between friends, is it time to end the friendship? While the rewards of friendship are endless, so, too, are the challenges.

I must admit, the pain of ending a friendship is my worst nightmare, even when the friendship is toxic. I have found it much easier to give up a husband or two than a girlfriend who often offends.

Ultimately, ending a bad friendship will make us a little happier and a lot healthier. My friend Anita Gutterman says, "It took me a lifetime to realize this, but once you begin to move forward with the friends who really count, it feels great to have unburdened yourself of those heavy emotional weights."

Research agrees with Anita. It shows that a stressful relationship with friends (or family for that matter) causes physical and emotional issues such as high blood pressure, risk of depression and anxiety.

And so I ask you: For which friend would you risk your health?

Here's my short list of justifiable deal breakers.

The Betrayer: breaking our confidence or intentional cruelty is so offensive that it's unlikely we would care to revive or renew a friendship after this breach.

The Headache: if an afternoon of conversation leaves you thinking, "Get me out of here," chances are there's something amiss. If you walk away feeling headachy, depressed, anxious, stressed or unhappy, it's best to see less—or nothing at all of this friend.

The Disappointer: she is always late, re-scheduling or fails to show at all. She adores you, but truly can't make the finish line. Respecting a friend's time is important and sends a message of fondness and fairness.

The Embarrassment: it's not her appearance; it's her behaviour. She often says something to embarrass you and perhaps others as well. Some folks do this on purpose while others are too simple to know. Shamers like Zella fall easily within this category.

The Jealous Giant: not everyone is comfortable with your success. Some friends are so insecure, they can't tolerate anyone else's win. These people are cringe-worthy. Their self-esteem is so low they're jealous of those who do and those who have. While courageous people are reaching their goals, cowards are criticizing the success and happiness of others.

After carefully examining a disappointing friendship, you may decide it's past its best before date. But I caution, if termination is the destination, it's a long drive back to reunion.

I am sure you'll agree that even the closest relationships experience the odd setback and are still worthy of revival. Few things affect us more deeply than a broken friendship. When people have touched our hearts, their absence leaves a void. And it hurts.

Friendships often stay broken because it's easier to let go than reach out. But don't let fear of rejection stand between you and a dear friend. If you want the friendship back, put yourself out there. Take the risk and reap the rewards.

Results may vary.

Not everyone has the ability to fix a friendship, but it's an admirable quality. A willingness to reach out and be vulnerable is a marvelous advantage.

I believe that every success serves up confidence, but every failure provides an opportunity for wisdom and growth.

CHAPTER THIRTY-TWO

It takes a village

FOLLOWING MY LESSON on Empathy, inmate Kyle stayed to chat. In a secretive whisper he said,

"Your lesson was interesting today, Phyllis, but I'm a narcissist."

Thankfully, I've trained myself not to blink. "Interesting, Kyle, take a seat."

"How do you know you're a narcissist?"

"I was told by my aunt a few years back. My mom's sister. She's a psychotherapist or something."

Being selfish from time to time is part of the human condition, but there is a big difference between having a selfish moment and being a callous narcissist.

Those rare people diagnosed with narcissistic personality disorder exhibit at least five of these symptoms:

An overactive sense of self-worth. A sense of entitlement.

Mental images of success, power, intelligence or beauty. An agenda that uses others.

A belief that they are special. A lack of empathy.

Association only with powerful people.	A belief that others envy them.
A forceful need for admiration.	An egotistical and arrogant attitude.

So you think you know a few of these critters? Not so fast. Even the above criteria doesn't guarantee a diagnosis—longevity factors in too.

Inmate Kyle wasn't ticking many boxes. At nineteen, he was a bit short and unusually slender. He had sapphire blue eyes and a pleasant enough face, surrounded by lots of blond hair. Kyle had a quirky personality and a smile that was delightful. At times I wondered if he worked at being a bit quirky.

Kyle never missed a class nor a chance to challenge my teachings, but his curiosity was respectful. He was intelligent, well-spoken and a deep thinker. I felt Kyle had potential, but he appeared not to like the others and never spoke with anyone except me.

Listening to Kyle label himself as a narcissist broke my heart. A branding of narcissism creates a low psychological benchmark, which makes healing even tougher. When we label someone, that's often all they live up to, or what they fall back on. But changing the story can peel away hopelessness. That's my approach to healing.

"So, Kyle, if I were to tell you my mom just died, how would you feel?"

"Nothing. I'd feel nothing," he said staring at me to emphasize his narcissistic leanings.

"Okay," I said pausing and hoping for a breakthrough.

What do"you suppose contributed to your lack of empathy, Kyle?"

"My parents," he said, looking shamefully away.

"What about your parents? Tell me more."

"I'm an only child. My parents are devout Christians. For them, everything is evil. They told me that even thinking the word hell would get me there."

"As a kid, I was nervous to think that word. It was always their fear of God speaking. Every word, everything was about God. Christian programming was all I was allowed to watch. I liked cartoons, but the only acceptable ones were those with bible stories."

"Kyle, what you're describing is limiting and quite severe."

"I was not allowed friends. And no one was allowed at my home."

"Kyle, before we continue, I want to share something. As you know, I'm Jewish. What you don't know is that I survived a religious and restricted childhood as well. I had a father who was militant and abusive . . . used religion as a weapon. So, a harsh beginning."

He looked at me. And I could sense him thinking: But you seem okay.

"Most often, a highly restricted childhood like yours and mine, well . . . it causes us to struggle later in life. And those struggles might play out in some nasty ways. Our childhood difficulties cause us to form certain ideals, quite often flawed.

"I'm not saying that our challenges were the same Kyle, and I would never compare the severity. But what I can say is that I relate to, and validate, your struggle. I understand it. I get the restricted entertainment options. But why no friends?"

"I was home-schooled, so no friends from school," he explained.

"But after school? Neighbourhood kids, playgrounds . . ."

"No. I was locked in my bedroom. When they let me out, I was locked into the backyard along with the dogs, four dogs. I saw no one. I was completely isolated and extremely lonely."

"I remember screaming at them, I wanted to talk to someone. I wanted to see people, have friends . . . But it was never allowed," he said resentfully.

"I'm so sorry, Kyle." He could see the pain on my face; an involuntary demonstration of empathy.

"In church, they sat on either side of me, making sure my head was buried in a bible.

Punishments were severe too, they used food. I would lose a meal or two . . . there was nothing else left [for them] to confiscate."

Children who are mild souls often had a narcissistic parent—or two. Raised by pathological parenting, under these conditions, children are victims of psychological abuse with a full range of tragic outcomes. Too many parents wound their children.

Kyle continued, "When I was fourteen, my father put a computer in my room. And then internet. He got me started with an online prayer group. At first it was great because I could chat with kids who were like me. And some who were normal.

"But then one of the guys taught me how to access porn sites. So when I was fifteen, I learned a bad way to have fun. And that's what got me in trouble."

Kyle's confession came with visible shame. He was in prison on charges relating to child pornography. While it's not necessarily illegal to watch porn, there are laws in Canada that restrict the fabrication and distribution of pornographic content. The Criminal Code of Canada also makes it an offence to possess, fabricate, advertise or distribute content that qualifies as child pornography. As it should.

My role is not to address his crime, but to assist in healing what brought him to offend. With Kyle's considerable intelligence and wisdom, I felt confident that we could move forward.

"You had no opportunity to make friends, Kyle," I confirmed. "And no opportunity to develop feelings for others. The only feelings you had were for your parents. And those were likely feelings of anger and resentment.

"Does that seem right, Kyle?"

"Yes," he whispered, "I didn't want to feel angry, but I was . . . every single day."

"The situation you experienced at home makes it challenging to form friendships later in life," I said.

"And I bet it feels strange to be living with all these guys. But between us Kyle, this does not make you a narcissist. It makes you a guy who hasn't been exposed to people and was never afforded the opportunity to develop emotional feelings that would include understanding and compassion."

"Would you agree?"

"I don't know."

"Fair enough. But would you work with me for the next few months until your release?" Kyle had a year and change left on his ticket.

"Yes," he said without hesitation. "What should I do?"

I thought for a moment.

"Okay, let's consider me friend number one. This week, I want you to engage with someone you might already feel a slight connection with. Someone you feel is making progress here. Good progress. Good behaviour. He will become friend number two. Sound reasonable?"

He looked puzzled. "But how do I do that? How do I engage?"

"Just start to chat with one of the guys until you feel comfortable. Just like you and I are chatting now. We're making friends right now, aren't we, Kyle?

With no words but his quirkiest smile, Kyle was saying 'yes.'

"Take your time. It will take a few days, maybe more. But when you feel a slight connection, ask the guy if he would like to sit with you at lunch, or play cards, or watch TV, whatever your privileges permit.

"It will feel a bit uncomfortable Kyle, but I'm asking you to push through. We're going for risk and reward here.

"You'll thank me," I said, and he nodded.

Kyle and I had struck an agreement.

Friendship is paramount to surviving prison. Having the connection and support of those who have been through similar traumas and challenging circumstances gives strength to the weary. Often, friendship begins the healing process. In prison, however, choosing the right friend can be a challenge.

But a week later, Kyle had made a friend. And then he made many friends, chatting easily with the guys about topics we covered on Motivational Mondays and other stuff. He smiled more often. I even saw Kyle deliver a friendly slap or two on an inmate's shoulder. Perhaps he was imitating the friendlier guys but it was working.

During this restorative process, Kyle and I would meet regularly for life coaching and encouragement. He was attending every available class, reading self-help books and doing really well. Everyone could see the change.

Kyle became less quirky and more like the guy everyone liked. He supported fellow inmates, making a clear effort to provide leadership and guidance. And as Kyle led, his intelligence shone. Whenever I mentioned him to another inmate they would chuckle and smile with pride. It's a very special club we've got at Ontario Correctional.

Being granted parole at the Ontario Correctional Institute is rare. In an unprecedented show of commitment, Kyle gave up his opportunity for early parole. He explained to me (and to others) that he was learning more in prison than he could ever hope to at home.

After Kyle had served his full time, he asked for mine. And began by preaching to the choir.

"Phyllis, friendship's a really good thing."

"You're kidding?" I joked, but with mentorship pride.

Significantly, Kyle was asking for guidance. He had decided to further his education, was exploring the possibility of becoming a counsellor, and hoping for an opportunity to work in the prison system.

"I want to do what you do, Phyllis," he said. "If it weren't for our talks, I would still be that loner, the kid with no friends. I believe in the stuff you do here."

Kyle was leaving prison to create a new life and wanted to be of service.

Three years later . . .

I entered the prison and heard someone running behind me.

"Hi there!" an enthusiastic, out of breath voice rang out.

Pivoting, I discovered Kyle in a charcoal trench coat carrying a briefcase. He had much less hair, but he still had remnants of that quirky smile. I was filled with glee. And kvelling. My heart bursts just thinking of this moment.

"Kyle!"

"Yes, Miss."

"What are you doing here?"

"I'm a case worker, Phyllis, hired a month ago. I was hoping to meet up. I've been asking about you."

"Kyle, I'm overwhelmed with joy."

"You didn't think I forgot about you?" He said with a warm smile.

I could sense the dignity and fulfillment that Kyle had rightly earned. He had made it.

"I'm ecstatic, Kyle, and so proud of you."

"How are things with you now? With you and your family?"

"Well, my parents and I still have the odd phone call but it's difficult now. Religion, it's just not my thing. We don't speak the same language, never have, and, since I've stepped back from the church, it seems there's no bridge to healing."

"I wish we could arrive at some mutual respect and understanding. I'm okay with it though.

Their religious beliefs and restrictions contributed to a bad outcome for me—not that I blame them. I was weak back then.

"Our connection will likely grow less over time. And that's okay too, I've moved on."

"Kyle, you're making wise choices, my friend."

"I have something else to tell you, Phyllis. Remember when you pushed me to make friends? At the time I thought it was . . . ah . . . ridiculous. But, I decided to give it a try. What you said to me four years ago was, 'You'll thank me.'"

"Today, I want to thank you, Phyllis. You gave me a life."

Although the capacity for empathy is inborn, it's a learned behaviour. Infants learn to identify and regulate their emotions by interacting with their parents. Parents who are receptive to their children's cues, permit their babies to thrive and develop emotional wellness.

When a baby's emotional state is responded to, the groundwork is laid, not just for the child's sense of self, but their sense of others. In time, this emotional wellness grows into empathy and forms a pathway for intimate connection. This is called secure attachment.

We underestimate the power of kindness. In Hebrew we have the word tzedakah which means charity, or good deeds. Many of us have the ability to influence the lives of others, encourage the weak and boost the struggling.

So what does it take? A belief in someone that goes deeper than their own. A word, despite adversity or resistance, that steers them in the right direction. A calm but constant coach, and a reminder that they can do more—and be more.

It takes a village.

CHAPTER THIRTY-THREE

Justice in the jungle

PRISONERS ARE A BLEND of humanity. Most come from dark places and have experienced excruciating pain. Their stories touch my heart in a way that encourages fearlessness. Their stories are personal. Our relationships are personal.

These people matter to me.

While I understand they are being punished for wrongful behaviour, I do what I can to make their lives hurt less as long as we remain within ethical boundaries—and a lesson is learned. That lesson is not necessarily directed at them.

"We've been wanting to speak with you for a few weeks now. Sort of waiting for the right time," Ken began.

After a lesson on Critical Problem Solving, Ken and a dozen other inmates requested a private moment. Something was going down.

Ken was fifty-something, tall with grey hair. A white collar guy who stood out from the crowd, he was always well groomed and had a managerial demeanour. Ken was confident, analytical and had impressive leadership qualities.

"What's up, guys?" I asked as we leaned into a huddle.

"Well, remember last week you were speaking about bullies. We've got one, and he is making life hell around here," Ken explained as everyone listened carefully.

In most prisons, guards are bullies. It's a fact of prison life. But at the Ontario Correctional Institute, the staff pride themselves on showing respect. It's a core value that they're expected to teach by example.

"I see, tell me more."

There's always a risk in getting involved, but my interest in mediating tends to win out. I may go out on some delicate limbs, but I begin by making the choice from solid grounds.

Bullying is never okay.

"So, boys, I'm here for you."

"Some of the guys are having a problem with Stillman, that heavy guard with the shaved head. No matter what we do with this guy, we can't win. We get into trouble for doing absolutely nothing most of the time."

I knew Stillman. He had a reputation as a hard-ass. "How many of you are experiencing this?"

"All of us. That's why we've asked for your guidance. We don't know what to do. Where to turn."

"Can you give me a specific example, Ken?"

"How did I know you'd ask? Last Sunday, Smiley was telling me a funny story about his girlfriend coming to visit. Don't ask me to repeat it though," he said, blushing slightly.

"Yeah . . ." I probed, curious about the girlfriend story but assuming it was just for mens' ears.

"Well, I began to laugh. I was laughing quietly for a long time. Stillman kept walking by and giving me a scowl like I shouldn't be laughing," Ken said with a deliberately puzzled look, palms up.

I will never forget Ken's unusually sad, piercing brown eyes.

"But laughing's good, and it's certainly permissible," I added in support.

"Nope. We got an infraction. Both of us, me and Smiley. It's always Stillman. He's rough on all of us for absolutely no reason. Never needs an excuse to be rude. Just hands out infractions and makes our lives hell."

"Last month, Joel got sent to "Seg" for nothing, and he came back in a serious state of depression. Some of us thought he might be suicidal and alerted the staff. He still continues with dangerous thoughts."

Several other inmates shared Stillman stories as well.

An infraction ticket can result in a variety of punishments depending upon the breach itself and the inmate's behavioural record.

Whatever the reasons for their incarceration, inmates are human beings who deserve respect, dignity and fair treatment. The Ontario Correctional Institute is meant to be a healing place and co-workers (guards and such), are answerable to one another. Respect and humanity are recognized as essentials and part of the healing journey.

Still, nasty finds its way through the cracks.

"Okay, guys. Let's make plans," I said slowly, raising my right arm in a gesture of victory.

Everyone nodded and their attention was on me.

For me, inspiration occurs when I believe in myself and others. I take it very seriously that inmates receive a fair shake. When I'm asked to find a solution, I hope for inspiration, but it can be scary. Sometimes there are no answers. But I had an idea that, with a prayer and a bit of luck, might work.

"So, guys, here's what we're gonna do. First, we need to agree that what's said in here, stays in here. More important than ever today, right?"

They nodded vigorously. With my group, loyalty is a given. We have a remarkable bond that's built on trust. I have never had any confidence come back to bite me. And it works both ways.

"Secondly, everyone needs to be in total agreement with my plan, or there is no plan. And you'll need to fill in the others."

They were smiling now with a what's she gonna do now? Look.

"Even if some of you don't like the plan, you're in. I repeat, this is an all or nothing membership proposal."

My strategy was to prep them for something big, when in fact the concept was simple. But it required discipline.

"A show of hands, guys."

Every hand was raised. Smiley raised both hands.

"Okay, here's the plan. Stillman's a bully. He's using his power for intimidation rather than motivation. I won't tolerate bullies. I ask that you fly under the radar for one full week until I return. Next week we will regroup and determine our next steps, depending on how it goes."

"Exactly how do you mean 'under the radar'?" Smiley asked.

"Good question, Smiley. First, you're all on best behaviour. And, where possible, you're going to avoid Stillman. But when he addresses you, you're to give only one of three acceptable responses: Yes, Sir. No, Sir. Thank you, Sir.

"You in?"

All the men smiled and nodded. Maybe Humpty Dumpty would have a great fall.

"Say nothing else," I insisted. "Our insurance policy is that no one speaks back to Stillman, no matter what."

As I paused, they repeated in unison, "No matter what!"

"Now, remember how we learned about body language? We need highly respectful body language here, just like I taught you in NLP. Everyone got it?"

Neuro-linguistic programming, as I've mentioned, is all about body language. It's a powerful communication tool that I teach to prisoners. Non-verbal communication conveys a significant portion of the messaging we send and receive and is valuable in how we understand, or fail to understand, others. It's especially helpful face to face and can make a critical difference when emotions or attitude is involved.

"Okay let's rehearse, guys," I said, standing up.

"I'll be Stillman, so someone show me how we say, 'Yes, Sir.'"

Victor stood up and, with his arms at his sides and his head pointed slightly up at a 10-degree angle, he responded with a calm and respectful voice. "Yes. Sir."

I sprang forward enthusiastically. "Guys, we have a plan! It's called: The Stillman Experiment."

There was excitement in the air as the men, chatting and laughing, left the room. That evening I headed home feeling excited and a little nervous. I had faith in the men for sure, but you never know what will happen. A week is a very long time.

This was my plan: If I arrived back at OCI to men reporting that their behaviour was stellar but someone had still received an infraction, I would take it to the authorities. And I would be speaking with conviction and the proof to persuade. I know how to make a point. Simply put, Stillman was a bully.

The following week, as planned, the group stayed after class to update me.

"Okay guys, what happened this week?"

Spokesperson Ken filled me in using his calm, professional-sounding voice. "Well, after five days of following your, 'yes sir, no sir, everything goes, sir' thing, Bob got an infraction. And then Joe did."

"Oh crap," I mumbled. "What for?"

"Bob hadn't done anything wrong, neither had Joe. We were all following The Stillman Experiment."

"Bob was chatting quietly with Mike on Saturday morning when Egghead [Stillman] came along and accused Bob of giving him attitude. It never happened and there were witnesses."

"And?"

"So, we held an emergency meeting during gym and decided to take things into our own hands."

I was nervous and proud at the same time.

"Enough of this shit, pardon my language, Phyllis. We left you out of it. After the Bob incident, me and the boys approached another guard."

Ken explained that Richardson, a young guard known for his fairness, reacted favourably. Hours later, he took the 13 men into a meeting with Stillman and confronted him.

Richardson and the boys told Stillman about "The Stillman Experiment" and, of course, their findings.

Thus challenged, Stillman actually admitted that he couldn't stand inmates laughing and blamed his impatience on a sticky divorce. He then reversed several of the more recent infractions.

By the time I arrived at the prison, Stillman had actually been fired. The men were exhilarated.

A strong code of silence persists among guards, which often results in recurrent excessive use of force or other forms of punishment. There's a social incentive for staff to conceal information or even lie to protect each other. There is a sick joke told by the staff of correctional institutions:

Question: How many officers does it take to push an inmate down stairs?

Answer: None. He fell.

But Richardson, ethical and fair, saved the day!

I am so grateful to work in an environment that respects respect. And happy to be of service to the mighty men in orange. I should mention, no prisoner has ever asked me to do anything that crosses the line.

And that's respect too.

CHAPTER THIRTY-FOUR

Anger matters

WHAT MAKES YOU ANGRY? For me, it's being dealt with unkindly, or witnessing an unkind act.

For many, a violation invokes a retaliation. No one wants to feel that their beliefs or feelings are being disrespected or disregarded.

In the prison system, anger is a serious topic—many criminal acts are carried out as a result of anger gone wrong.

But let's not make the mistake of thinking that a life of anger is preordained when there are prevention techniques proven to work. With deeper insight into our triggers and some mind-blowing combat hacks (make that habits), we can wage a war on anger. And win.

While anger is a natural emotion, chronic anger is not. Anger looks and feels bad, and it trails nightmares that keep us up at night.

In researching anger years ago, I learned that it can be addictive. That's right, the adrenalin rush we get from anger contributes to a sense of invincibility. This explains those Kung Fu Fighters we know who engage and enrage at the slightest provocation.

Out of control anger can easily destroy families and ruin lives. People on the receiving end of anger develop fear, resentment and a lack of trust. Although lashing out may feel justified, it leaves emotional damage in its wake.

Some people have a hair trigger temper. You may know a few of these barking dogs: narcissists, constant competitors, and those with low tolerance and limited patience are in the pack. And yes, anger may run in families— genetics play a role—but experiences in early childhood are equally, if not mostly, to blame. Experts see anger as a learned behaviour; a response to, or symptom of, something else. It could be anything from pain, hunger, tiredness or humiliation to bigger issues like grief, failure, infidelity or sexual frustration.

You should see the inmates try not to snicker when I discuss sexual frustration. Maybe they're trying to tell me something.

We all get angry from time to time. Even an irritation like boredom may cause low-level anger, often referred to as frustration. The idea is to get ahead of the anger and stop the escalation before we lose the ones we love. The physical ramifications are scary. Studies show that for two hours following an anger outburst, there's a higher risk of chest pain (angina), heart attack, stroke or a risky heart rhythm. Would you sign up for these risks?

My three year old granddaughter thinks Timeout is hide and go seek, but it's a bit different for us. Timeout involves leaving a situation when we feel our anger escalating or stopping ourselves when we feel our inner badass engaging. When you're in heat (no, not mating—anger), either call a timeout or throw up the timeout hand signal. This lets others know that a topic change would be better than a verbal brawl. Be careful with that hand signal, though, not all signals carry the same meaning.

In heightening our anger awareness, let's use an anger meter: one or two represents cool; readings between 3 and 9 represent rising anger; and 10 represents heat. Heat is out of control anger which results in screaming or assault—so behaviour that carries consequences.

When we experience an anger event, we don't instantly spike. There is a moment between anger setting in and behaviour playing out. Using that escalation time to reduce our anger response is crucial.

(In the next chapter, I introduce tough Tony, incarcerated for a brutal assault. My boy Tony learned that choice is a real thing. It still makes me smile thinking of Tony and the boys of Maplehurst manor.)

The key objective of anger management is to keep our anger reading as low as possible and circumvent going nuts. At times, specific events invoke our sensitivities. These inflammatory little suckers are referred to as triggers. We all have them, but what triggers me, might be cotton candy for you.

An important component of hacking anger is the ability to identify the signals that warn us when we're about to blow. These signals fall into four categories: physical, behavioural, emotional and cognitive.

A physical signal is how our body responds when we become angry. Our heart may pound, we may feel lightheaded or flushed. These are warning signs that anger is on the horizon.

A behavioural signal is the conduct we display. We might pace, slam doors, break dishes or slowly raise our voices. (I do voice.) These behavioural responses are second level anger signals and a warning that we're approaching blast off.

A primary emotion is what we feel immediately before an anger event. Common triggers are pain, hunger, frustration, tiredness, stress and more. These are the core feelings that underlie anger. An important aspect of breaking the anger cycle is being aware of and recognizing these primary feelings. And having a plan to avoid nasty outbursts.

The last signal, cognitive, is what we think in response to the event. At times, our mind will interpret a person's comment as criticizing, humiliating or controlling and we do that at lightning speed. Sadly, our anger escalates quickly and often without real cause.

There is no one size fits all fix, but there are anger control techniques to get you started. In developing an anger control plan, the idea is to try on different bits and see what works.

I find it effective to discuss my anger with a fair and frank friend. Pick a confidential person to help you determine if your thoughts and expectations are rational. Remember, there will always be other perspectives. (If you don't agree, please consider joining Egotists Anonymous.)

When I discuss my issues with friends, I come away with an alternative view of the situation and a deeper understanding. The opportunity to express our feelings with a good listener is cathartic and encourages wisdom.

Anecdotally, studies suggest that there are unique perspectives between the sexes and it's important to factor this in as well.

We know that self-talk (your inner voice) is a welcome and easily accessible tool. Calm yourself down by shifting your focus from blame to understanding and compassion. At times, the anger freak eagerly escalates, only to find out later that the outburst was not based on fact.

When feeling anger, pausing is our personal antidote. You can pause. I mean, what's the rush? Wait before contacting a person who you think did you some dirt.

It's impossible to be angry and relaxed at the same time. If you can relax a bit, you will approach the situation with more sanity and control.

Compassion inoculates us against feelings of anger. If we believe that what someone did to anger us was unintentional, it's easier to de-escalate and decompress. If we apply a smidge of compassion, we have an excellent path to control. By habitually thinking more compassionately and less judgmentally, we trade angry bits for compassionate wits.

When we master a compassionate mind, calmness will prevail.

In the prison system, assaultive or violent behaviour is associated with anger. I am very proud that my anger management hacks are seen as sound treatment for the ragers, haters and abusers among violent offenders.

Prisoners reported experiencing a reduction in anger when using the following techniques, and perhaps you will too.

Cognitive Therapy Techniques
Simmering Your Anger
Close your eyes and get comfortable.
Think of a situation when you were angry.
Get in touch with the feelings you had during the anger event.

Allow yourself to feel, hear and see the event unfolding.

Imagine placing your anger into a pot of boiling water.

The water boils over and spills out onto the oven, countertop and the floor.

Follow the boiling water as it flows out over the floor.

Envision the water flowing farther and farther out.

As the water spreads across the floor, feel it becoming cooler and cooler.

The water is no longer hot, nor is your anger.

Imagine yourself feeling the cool waters.

Do not rush your feelings, stay here for a moment or two.

Keep spreading the water across the floor until it completely evaporates.

Open your eyes.

I asked "twelve angry men" to invoke this technique the next time they became angry. Several men reported experiencing a significant drop in anger.

Gaining New Perspective

Repeat steps 1-4 above.

Try to find a different perspective by asking yourself: What would Billy think? (Where Billy is an intelligent and reasonable guy.)

Repeat, replacing Billy with others, until you have a different perspective.

Open your eyes.

The Thought Stopper

Stop the "hot thought" on the spot. Instead of analyzing your thoughts and beliefs, stop the thought before an escalation of anger takes hold. Replace the angry thought with your favourite place to be, or a person you choose to be with.

Mantra Madness

Find a phrase that calms you down just long enough to refocus (try "rolling waves"). Repeat the mantra to yourself until you feel calmness set in.

Setting Intentions

Set deliberate intentions to focus on your highest aspirations. This helps you to connect with what is most meaningful, where anger is not an option. Set your intentions both before sleep and again upon waking. You're committing to striving for your desired achievements.

In prison, we apply the intention setting technique to anger management and all sorts of addictive and behavioural challenges.

Journaling

When anger is setting in, remove yourself from the situation and make notes. Record the situation and how you intend to handle it in a way that will move you closer to your goals.

Processing thoughts through journaling calms us down and provides an opportunity to assess. In prison, I remind inmates of their aspirations to reunite with family, especially when they are striving for a parenting opportunity.

Trigger Rehearsing

Rehearsal before an actual event provides a safe but imaginary role play opportunity. To prevent a ghastly outburst, rehearse how you're going to manage the situation by imagining appropriate behaviour.

Plan several possible scenarios and arrive feeling confident and prepared.

Physical Relaxation Techniques

The following physical relaxation techniques can be performed separately or in combination with one another.

Breathing

Begin to focus on your breathing.

Take a deep breath in to the count of 4.

Hold it for seven seconds.

Now exhale fully to the count of 8.

Repeat several times until you feel fully relaxed.

Hands

Bring awareness to your hands.

Clench your fists very tightly.

Hold that tension for a few seconds.

Now relax your fists, letting your fingers unfold slowly and letting your hands completely relax.

Repeat several times until you feel fully relaxed.

Arms

Bring awareness to your arms.

Curl your arms as if you are doing a bicep curl.

Tense your fists, forearms, and biceps.

Hold that tension for a few seconds.

Now release the tension in your arms slowly and allow your arms and hands to rest.

Feel the tension drain out of your arms.

Repeat several times until you feel fully relaxed.

Shoulders

Raise your shoulders toward your ears.

Tense your shoulders.

Hold them up for a few seconds.

Gently drop your shoulders and release the tension.

Now bring awareness to your neck and face.

Repeat several times until you feel fully relaxed.

When we manage anger we develop peace. Crashing waves become innocuous ripples. Many who practice meditation, yoga and mindfulness speak of an inner sanctuary without which they would never survive.

Life is grand when we are not occupied with thoughts of victimization. We must pause to understand, rather than rush to rage. Then we can consider our choices and choose wisely. Because every word and every action will matter.

CHAPTER THIRTY-FIVE

"I smash his head"

"Correctional institutions are attempting to reduce violence in prison by offering anger management programs. It is also hoped that these programs will curb aggressive behaviour after release. As a result, programs for anger management have implications for both prison management and broader society." – Correctional Service of Canada.

MAPLEHURST CORRECTIONAL INSTITUTE, a high security prison for men, commissioned me to write a book on Anger Management and deliver the course. The attendees were serving time for violent acts of aggression and were mandated by the courts to receive training. Upon completion of my course, each inmate would receive an Anger Management Certificate.

I was given a stack of rap sheets (criminal records) and told to select a dozen prisoners who would benefit from my course. Since it was literally impossible to pick, I was essentially asked to play God. Nevertheless, I made the selections and was given twelve angry men, a sleepy guard, and a big blue panic button. My personal agenda was to cultivate kindness.

And I did. Four weeks into the course, however, we learned something about anger management, courtesy of my guy Tony.

"Miss, I like you. You're nice 'n all, but this anger management stuff, it ain't for me. I know we gotta take yer class 'n all but, I mean, I'm just a real angry guy."

"If a guy does me dirt, I just bash hiz head in . . . end a story."

"I've always been like this, ain't nothin' gonna change that. Courts say we gotta learn anger stuff 'n all, but it don't work on me. No one can fix this wicked anger."

Now that was a lovely speech "'n all," but when my men go low, I go teach.

"Tony, I understand exactly what you're telling me. And you know what? You're making a good point about your automatic response. As I explained last week, my friend, some people are born angrier than others. But we can all learn to buy time, calm down and gain control. Right?"

"Sure Miss, but not me." He announced with confidence. "Some guy fucks wit' me, I hurt em. It's real simple. Sorry for swearin' Miss."

And that was my opening. Tony only taking about men who made him angry. And he was apologizing to a women for swearing.

"Tony, can you give me an example of when someone disrespected you and how you lost it."

Tony barely thought about it. "Well, what got me here. My apprentice."

"Would you share your story with us, please Tony?"

"Yeah, sure. I'm a mechanic. I own a small auto body shop in town. Carlos, he whaz my apprentice. Carlos whaz learnin' from me and that would get 'im his work papers. Papers he needed to be a certified mechanic."

"One day, I told 'im. I said, 'Carlos, I'm goin' ta lunch. See this car here I've bin workin' on? Don't touch nothin' till I get back. You touch it, you'll break it. It's all messed up. And Carlos said, 'sure boss.'"

"So, I come back from lunch and Carlos sez ta me, 'Ay boss, I know you told me not to touch that car but I thought I'd finish up while you whaz out 'cause I need to leave early taday. But somethin' went sorta wrong.'"

"Oh gosh Tony, what happened?"

"Well, whaddaya think happen? Carlos—he touch the car, he broke it. I couldn't fix it no more.

So, I was out a lotta money. The car whaz toast and Carlos whaz jam."

"Oh my God, Tony. I certainly understand your anger. What did you do?"

"Well, I warn 'im not to touch. That was fair, right?"

"So I smash his head. I smashed his head up against the car—just 'til he got the message.

"And it got me a deuce at Maplehurst. Assault causing bodily [harm]."

I would find out later that Carlos sustained minor heard injuries.

I also learned more about angry Tony's background. His parents were drug addicts who fought one another for a fix. They would lock him and his young brother Eddie outside, sometimes for hours, even in horrid weather. At the tender age of five, physical and emotional abuse had already begun. The family lived in tents, cars and on people's floors until Tony was ten. By age fourteen, Tony and his girlfriend Sarah had left home and found their own tent.

Months later, Sarah's parents found the couple under a bridge just west of the Humber Trail, north of Toronto. Grateful for their safety, Sarah's parents took the pair home to reside. Sarah's dad was an auto mechanic who gave Tony his first break. Tony and Sarah are long since married with a son who's a criminal lawyer. Life is grand.

Tony and I continued the anger debate.

"Tony, that's so unfortunate. You were provoked, so you lost your temper and ended up in the Hurst. I get it. But do you think you might have handled it a bit differently? Maybe avoided prison?"

"Nope. I have no control over my anger, Miss. None. I burst in ta flames and that's it. Over. No time to think. I'm in and outta here like I own seasons tickets. That's me, prison ain't no big deal."

And then he said, "Good roof, good bed, good God, I'm fed." And all the guys chuckled. Perhaps a theme song? But so interesting how one man's heaven is another man's hell.

Having told his story, Tony acted as if he'd won a special courage award instead of a jail term.

I paused and slowly looked around the room. The guys were watching me and smiling. You could easily interpret their look as: we all have a Tony Story.

Okay, they think I have no idea. I'll show them how we turn a question into a lesson.

"Tony." I said slowly and then paused. "Thank you for sharing your story with us and for being so open and honest. You know how I appreciate honesty, and I appreciate people who are willing to work on their anger too. Do you think we could do a little work today, Sir?"

"Sure," he said, up for a challenge.

Taking a deep breath, I was hoping no one would notice that I was nervous as hell. But I'd seen my chance earlier. It was time to play the lady card.

"Tony, what if the same thing happened at the auto body shop, but rather than Carlos being your apprentice, it was your mom. So, you go to lunch, you tell your mom not to touch the car, and she does. It breaks. What would you do to your mom, Tony?"

"Oh fuck, not my mom. I would never hurt my mom, eh. Love Mom."

"Well then, Tony," I continued, "What if it were me? What if . . . what if I were your apprentice?"

"No. I wouldn't hurt you, Miss. I like you too much." And he smiled like he was proud to be human.

"Whoa Tony, you just taught us all something really cool. You told us that you wouldn't hurt your mom, nor would you hurt me. Is that correct?" I spoke slowly, hoping to let it sink in.

"Correct," he said, beaming with chivalry.

"Damn, Tony, that's astonishing!" Twelve angry men were about to have an awakening. "Tony, listen. This is mind-blowing!"

At this point the men were looking at me like I'd left my brain cells in a security locker.

"From time to time you are triggered. But between the trigger event and the time you perform an action, an out of control anger action, Tony, you . . . have . . . a moment to decide what to do!"

"As you said, you wouldn't hurt your mom, nor would you hurt me. That proves that there's time, a very brief moment of time between your thoughts and your actions. It's what I've been calling the escalation period. The anger meter, Tony. Remember the anger meter?"

"You have that brief moment to make a choice—control it or lose it. The escalation period cuts us a break. Do you see this opportunity? Do you see how you have time to make a choice?" I was speaking excitedly, hoping my enthusiasm wasn't embarrassing him.

Tony now seemed less proud and more aware. Actually, he was pondering my findings. And as my nervousness began to flow into calm, we were smiling at one another.

"Guess so," he said with a peaceful demeanour rarely seen in this angry group.

"So, Tony, today you taught us that we have a window of opportunity. A period of time when we can decide our course of action before we act out. Agree?"

"Yes," Tony said decisively, with a proud look of enlightenment.

It was a pivotal moment.

"Men, what do you think? Did Tony teach us something valuable today? Everyone gets angry, but we have options. Each of us can make the choice to control our anger and stay out of prison. What do you think, guys?"

The inmates, armed with a bit more knowledge, nodded in unison and smiled.

They had a moment of awareness and I had a moment of gratitude.

Nowadays, I never teach anger management without telling this, my Tony Story.

While attending the final class, I felt a bit deflated that our time was coming to an end. Anger Management is an eight-week course. I would be delivering the last lesson and then handing out their coveted Anger Management Certificates.

As Tony entered the class, I noticed he was carrying a paper. And smiling like he'd won the lottery. After everyone was seated, the guys couldn't contain themselves. Something was up.

"Weez got somethin' for ya today, Miss," Tony said, beaming.

With enormous confidence and self-respect, Tony presented me with his personally handcrafted, coffee-stained, Certificate of Institution which read:

"For completing the task of putting up with us for eight session introductory program that helps participants develop practical attitudes, thinking, and beliefs."

My Certificate of Institution was signed by Tony and his cellmate Jeff.

I was overwhelmed with emotion, gratitude and pride. A single tear rolled down my cheek as I realized that twelve angry men had gotten together to create a meaningful and deeply touching award for my efforts.

"Weez got yer back, Miss," Tony said.

Uncontrolled anger is detrimental to our health and a danger to others. Let us all learn from Tony that we have a choice. Anger can be controlled.

If you're on this journey with me, try the techniques described in the previous chapter and determine what works best for you. But, if your anger issues are out of control, cause regrets or hurt others, please seek counselling today.

There is help out there and no reason to get stuck on anger.

CHAPTER THIRTY-SIX

Intentional happiness

ARE YOU PASSIONATE about life?

Happiness is an emotion that falls somewhere between contentment and bliss. Joy is deeper than happiness—I say it's felt in the soul. While happiness can be experienced with a good meal and good neighbours, joy is living your best life.

My pursuit of joy is no accident.

In navigating my personal challenges, dosing with happy allows me to store positive emotional energy in order to survive the emotional pain that living a full life presents. The goal is to create a reservoir of strength.

I like to do lunch.

Happiness, in part, is genetic. Studies show the heredity factor to be about 50 per cent. Yes, about half of our capacity to experience happiness can come from Mom and Dad.

Happiness is tricky though. I've weathered many serious setbacks and each cloud came with a bright silver lining, but . . . Silver linings can only be seen when we're willing to expand our vision.

The truth is, the story we tell ourselves and the choices we make, matter. Because immense power lies in our thoughts.

What are your first waking thoughts?

For many of us, it goes like this: What's going on?

And then: What's going on in my day?

Blissed out happiness is hard to achieve. But not to worry, there are degrees of happiness that range between the bliss of exuberance and the despair of depression.

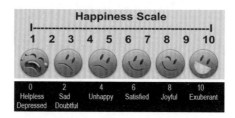

As we begin to envision our day, we establish a happiness setting. Provided that we are physically and emotionally well, our happiness setting should click in somewhere between five and seven. Conversely, when we are struggling or doing poorly (like my prison folk), our setting is significantly lower.

As we go through the day, stuff happens, causing our happiness setting to sink and soar. When we do lunch together, our happiness setting soars. Conversely, when we experience setbacks, our happiness setting sinks. The idea is to keep our happiness readings as high as possible. It's that reservoir thing.

When my first marriage ended without notice, there were a few dark days. Actually, every cell in my body was vibrating with fear. Finding myself alone with two toddlers and three mortgages was shitty. And on a wieners and beans budget, it was more than sad. It was terrifying. With this mess, I could either sink into a depression or float myself happy. For me, with two children who needed a mom and a lawyer who needed a clerk, there was no choice.

Clearly, I pulled myself up.

Two things needed to happen. First, I had to choose happy over sad. And then I needed to figure out exactly what happy was for me.

I determined that I wanted one of those loving-partners I had read about, but they don't grow on trees. But I figured that if I narrowed the search to planet earth, I could date like Cinderella. Little did I know that a few not-so Prince Charmings later, I would have broken glass slippers and a damaged heart.

Happiness is affected by many factors.

Passion and Purpose

Over the last decade, my work in the prison system has kept me afloat—cloud nine afloat. Actually, never mind clouds. The correctional system became my place in the sun.

You, too, must find your passion.

A sense of purpose provides meaning and direction. With purpose, each day becomes an expression of our identity. It manifests in a feeling of achievement that's wrapped in a very full heart. Pursuing joy is a commitment to do the things we genuinely love—regardless of obstacles and temptations. For me, it's writing and speaking. And lunching at The Cheesecake Factory.

Relationships

If you're serious about happiness, examine your relationships. All of them.

Fulfilling relationships have a positive influence on our lives. No shocker, right? People with satisfying relationships are found to have better health, higher sustained happiness, accelerated healing (or was that heating) and longer lives. Quite a package! Fortunately, these benefits are not limited only to intimate relationships. Even cuddles with Noodle the Poodle decrease stress and increase happiness.

Conversely, a struggling relationship is like black smoke blocking a sunny day. It messes with happiness. The excess stress of a relationship struggles release cortisol, disrupt immune and cardiovascular function and mess with mental health.

And physical healing takes longer too when we're in relationship hell. Been there.

Sleep

Some people think that they can cut sleep to accommodate work. Not so fast. Research says: no way. Nothing kills productivity and happy faster than a sleepless night. Research confirms that sleep is essential at any age. Sleep renews the mind, restores the body and is prescribed for healing and health. But how much sleep do we need for this optimum mind-body function? The National Sleep Foundation advises that healthy adults require between 7 and 9 hours of sleep per night.

So sleep well, folks, and wake up ready to rock!

Resiliency

Have you ever turned lemons into lemonade? I prefer lemon pie. Don't think magic—think magical. Losing the battle does not mean losing the war. Creating opportunities is the formula for bouncing back. We are not born resilient, but we can build resiliency through decisions that force us to accept and rebuild.

How long should we spend on yesterday?

A setback is a call to action. We must build, re-build and stack the deck in our favour. Then, celebrate the smallest of wins. Although moving on is difficult and even painful at times, you get to author this life! Through choices.

Resiliency is our ability to manage and recover from nasty and negative events. I have risen from catastrophe a few times only to emerge stronger, more confident and far more resilient. Having survived some hard blows, I learned to believe in myself and set out to fulfill my goals. We must strive to land on our feet.

I landed in prison!

Positive Thinking

Getting to a happier life begins and ends with our thoughts. Most of us have a running inner dialogue: small voice, big commentary. What we think determines how we feel. For best results, our internal talk track should be more boom and less gloom. And this is a learned function too.

Subconscious programming means that when experiencing a negative thought, you put that thought on trial. We can neutralize these little buggers by choosing to manifest calm. Examine each negative thought and reframe it by adding a pinch of positivity. We don't need to get too crazy now—just enough optimism for hope.

Among sophisticated positive thinking gurus, positive affirmations (I am tolerant, I am courageous, etc.) are common and calming chants. An experienced chanter will throw in a measure of music and dance on a stormy day.

Confidence

As a five-star extrovert, I've always wondered how 'shy' felt. Years ago while researching happiness, I found a link between extroversion and joy. This is not to say that introverts are unhappy. But studies show that if you tend to be introverted, simply acting like an extrovert can heighten happiness. I call that getting involved.

Confident people like who they are and radiate energy and enthusiasm. We all know those folks who walk in and light up a room.

So, raise a goblet of enthusiasm my friends and enjoy a happier you.

Introverts have significant advantages too. They tend to be excellent problem solvers, have greater academic achievements, impressive self-discipline and are less likely to take risks that affect safety.

Now that we've established my extreme extraverted markers, it's important to point out that it's rare to find either an extreme extrovert or an extreme introvert. Most folks fall betwixt the two. This means there are times when we need some crowd crazy and times when alone feels best. Either way, there's serious joy to be found in a warm bath or a cool book.

Interestingly, after our two-hour marathon chat, my friend Karen Sokoloff reported needing a nap, while I felt refreshed and rejuvenated. Different strokes.

Gratitude

Happiness does not make us grateful. Gratitude makes us happy. But we tend to get so comfortable with life that we forget to remember our bounty. Some people take life for granted, assuming that health and wealth is a certainty. But we must stop and sniff the abundance as we breathe in the excitement of life.

Stumbling upon this quote, I thought it encapsulated the full meaning of gratitude:

"There are only two ways to live your life. One is as though nothing is a miracle and the other is as though everything is a miracle."

Kindness

Do you believe in random acts of kindness? The act of doing good deeds without obligation, expectation or personal agenda? Of course you do. Because with goodness, we experience the warm wash of well-being. In fact, acts of kindness are so therapeutic that they're now being encouraged at your local psychotherapy clinic.

The science behind feel-better kindness, centres mostly on oxytocin. Sometimes called the love hormone, oxytocin plays a role in forming bonds and trusting people. It's the hormone mothers produce when they breastfeed, cementing a bond with their baby.

Oxytocin is also released when we're physically intimate and is tied to trust, generosity, and kindness, while lowering blood pressure. Hey, that's a smashing deal.

A year ago, my daughter created a Facebook group for local moms. The rules were clear. A mom could join with three simple restrictions. There would be no personal advertising, no drama and no charge for gently used baby or toddler wear. Within two hours, Melanie had 350 members. A year later, she had over a thousand members. Melanie proudly reports that her moms enjoy free clothing, toys and equipment as well as a measure of understanding, compassion and support that cannot be experienced elsewhere.

Not long ago, one devastated mom reported a fire in her home. She lost absolutely everything. Posting her frightening and heart-breaking situation for emotional support, within two hours moms were gathering up stuff and dads were dropping it off. Heartwarming for the receivers— and the givers.

Research, led by Professor of Medicine Steven Cole, PhD. found that people who have high levels of what is known as eudaimonic well-being (the kind of happiness that comes from having a deep sense of purpose and meaning in life) showed very favorable gene-expression profiles in their immune cells. This group had low levels of inflammatory gene expression and strong expression of antiviral and antibody genes. However, people who had relatively high levels of hedonic well-being (the type of happiness that comes from consummatory self-gratification) showed just the opposite. They had an adverse expression profile involving high inflammation and low antiviral and antibody gene expression.

Contagious Emotions

Many of us have experienced a mood swing via social media and at times it feels awful. The fear of missing out on something (or FOMO) keeps many of us coming back for our social media fix. Personally, I worry that I might offend someone if I don't like, share, or respond to the simplest party time post. When actually, most media users don't track and don't care.

While I consider myself a fairly positive poster, occasionally I can't resist a hot post. But before I do, I check my happiness reservoir to ensure it's not running on fumes. We can engage in any discussion when we set boundaries for comfort and care. My friends take sides on numerous divides. My goal is to render a respectful opinion, and consider the perspective of others.

A rainbow of intelligent viewpoints creates an exciting chat.

While you might think this is Pollyanna speak, my blood pressure remains quite stable and so do my friendships. The goal is to voice a view without ever angering an ally.

Validation and Approval

As I began working in the prison system, one friend said, "You're nuts risking your life," while another emphatically added, "You can't teach prisoners a damn thing."

I care what others think, but their opinions no longer hold me back. Striving for acceptance and validation is universal. After all, we evolved from tribalism to a global collective, where trust and respect mark success. Our need to belong is innate.

So, caring what others think is pretty normal. But if seeking the approval of others is a singular and debilitating focus, then what they think becomes more important than what we think. We must stop allowing Facebook, Instagram, Twitter, and phone friends to rule. Cut them loose. Do what's good for you.

Loneliness

We are not well-equipped for loneliness.

Douglas Nemecek, MD, chief medical officer for behavioral health, at Cigna, a US health insurer, reported that loneliness has the same impact on mortality as smoking fifteen cigarettes a day, making it even more dangerous than obesity.

Even social media with its high gloss version of life is a path to socialization and recommended for housebound folk.

"In the absence of love and belonging there is always suffering," says Brené Brown.

Anxiety and Fear

In his commencement speech at Yale University, actor Tom Hanks pointed out that fear spreads faster than gossip and is far more profitable. Fear, he told the graduates, will get the worst of the best of us.

Anxiety is ongoing, everyday fear.

Our insecurities can be based on fiction, not fact. But it doesn't let up, does it? It may even cause inappropriate behaviour. In order to achieve calm, look within and decide whether you need more facts or more confidence.

Fear, especially of failure, can be paralyzing. It moves us away from pleasure by destroying the confidence we need to explore our dreams. Allowing fear to hold us back, narrows our choices and the chance of attaining our goals.

Hate

Hate works much the same way. Filled with anger, pessimism and hostility, hate haemorrhages happiness. It screams inward and outward. Some life experiences are painful and recovery is slow and difficult. But making decisions based on hate either immobilizes us or sets us on a dangerous path.

Yoga, meditation and mindfulness are lifelines. For a lifetime of Zen, replace hostility with kindness. I promise that life will change.

Change

Change is a challenge for some and exciting for others. But for everyone, the bigger the change the greater the impact. Emotional gambles come with fear and uncertainty. However, at times we must make a change whether we like it or not.

Listen, the ability to imagine oneself thriving in a new situation is, as my prisoners say, "dope." If you're considering a life altering change: assess the impact, plan ahead, make the move.

You can always course correct.

The Misery Seeker

Most of us move toward pleasure and away from pain, but we all know a misery seeker. Gloom is their fashion statement. Even when presented with three easy steps to success, they see only limitations. With a preference for complaints over solutions, The Misery Seeker refuses to even think about the possibility of a positive outcome.

Jealousy

Jealously zaps the hell outta happy.

While it's normal to feel a smidge of jealousy (overwhelming insecurity over potential loss or inequity), or even a tinge of envy (longing for the advantages of others), fixating on what may be lacking in our lives causes emotional discomfort, diminishes relationships, and generally darkens the sky.

There will always be many with more. But is it really more? No one knows what's behind closed doors.

Shift your focus. Replace jealousy with desire to determine your personal passion. When used wisely, jealousy can be a powerful indicator and motivator in moving towards our goals.

So, what drives jealousy?

We all know that few things ruin bliss faster. Jealousy thrives in an environment of mistrust, the petri dish that breeds bad. Mistrust is a demon, delivering a constant stream of disturbing thoughts. Those thoughts feel so effing real.

A reality check is helpful, and so is courage to cope.

Body Image

A lifelong struggle with weight loss has tethered my happiness to the bathroom. The bathroom scale, that is. Turns out it's not just me. Media and advertising have promoted unrealistic standards of beauty that cause many to drop and drool.

Wipe the drool off your face my friends, and replace it with self-love and self-care. Researchers have discovered that dissatisfaction with our bodies diminishes happiness. And ya know what suffers? Everything from sex drives to confidence vibes.

I vote for a calorie free world, where weight doesn't even exist. Not that I'm moving anytime soon, but how about outer space?

Prince Charming

Another hindrance to happiness is a stop-at-nothing hunt for Mister Perfect. I can relate.

When you find the right person for you—someone who makes you feel seen, safe, and secure—quit the search and feel the love.

Patty Past

Do you know Patty Past? She never got over the husband who left her—thirty years ago. And, oh, Patty bought a necklace in Nassau and forgot to pick up the earrings. Poor Patty.

There is nothing gained by obsessing over a bad decision or a nasty ex-husband. A loss is a lesson called wisdom. We destroy any chance of future happiness if we're stuck in the back row of life. Why focus on past failures that were unwise, risky or tough? You survived, already.

For healing to happen, be mindful of now and look only towards the sun.

The Control Freak

Let me be blunt, trying to govern everything will result in an epic fail. A dictator manufactures their own disappointment and constant anxiety. It's self-destructive and causes extreme discomfort.

There are three spheres of control: that which we can control; that which we have influence over;

that which we can do nothing about. The goal is to recognize what we can't control and then step away. Sure, it's easier to figure out the issues than to let them go. But worrying over control raises our anxiety level to nuts.

Because the control freak can't control their anxiety, they try to control others. But when they realize that they can't even direct traffic, they become crazy and cruel. At times they feel resentment or even, God forbid, rage.

When things don't go as planned to the last detail, control freaks beat themselves up. In more extreme cases, these vexatious villains berate and belittle others, often without provocation or cause.

Get over yourself.

Expectations

Expectations are an invitation to disappointment and leave no room for creation, innovation or negotiation. Everyone suffers a setback, but we suffer less when we keep our expectations realistic.

Studies now show that if we strive for happiness like our lives depend on it, we end up chasing happy away. How? With thoughts and behaviours that are desperate and choices that are just all wrong.

Have you heard that life isn't fair? Watch how some people float through a situation that screams with adversity while others cave to a whispered "no." Disenchantment is tied to expectations, the little hellions that forcefully tamp down happy.

Face it folks, happiness is subjective. While some base their joy on the material, others value trust and loving connections. I say we embrace life with an open heart and an outstretched hand. Treat ourselves kindly, and treat others that way too.

Happiness is not magic, it's magical, and small steps make it happen.

CHAPTER THIRTY-SEVEN

One hand two hearts

APPINESS ISN'T ISSUED, it's earned. We create it intentionally and, when necessary, through blood, sweat, and fears. And that is precisely what Fariba, a young Iranian woman, did.

Iran executes more prisoners than virtually any other country (we don't know about China's numbers). The United Nations branded Iran's high number of death sentences "troubling."

Tens of thousands of political prisoners are jailed in Iran on various charges including advocating for democracy and promoting the rights of women, workers and ethnic minorities.

Droves of desperate people flee bullets, torture and imprisonment in Iran each year. Iranian women are often not expected to work. Treated as second class citizens, most women stay home, raise children and tend house. Their first language is Farsi (known also as Persian), but some have a working knowledge of English.

Prior to working in the prison system, I worked for years at an international law firm. Well into my tenure, I clocked out for two years to take a job teaching a paralegal course. The career college, which I won't name here, was privately owned and selfishly run.

Privately owned and operated colleges are generally smaller and more expensive than community colleges. In Ontario, these private learning centres focus their curriculum on specific career opportunities.

Private colleges attract a unique crowd; a full spectrum of students. Along with university grads, who are turning degrees into professions, there are welfare and unemployment fund recipients. Some of these students are eager, but in my experience many attend only for the purpose of collecting a government issued cheque. They're easy to spot. That is, when they make it to class.

Fariba, the young Iranian woman, enrolled in my course. The mother of twin teen girls, she was a mysterious, young lady in her mid-thirties. She had a sleek black pageboy, violet blue eyes and a stunning figure. With her beauty and bold enthusiasm, Fariba would ignite my day.

In contrast to Fariba's exquisite looks, she had a disfiguring injury. In place of her left hand was a prominent silver hook. She had lost her hand in Iran during a mass protest against tyranny, dire economic times and religious propaganda.

Fariba and her family (husband, the twins and both sets of grandparents) settled in Canada in a tiny apartment in Toronto's west end. Fariba longed to pursue an education, but her family felt that would be a waste of money. They constantly reminded her that she was unemployable by pointing at her awkward hook. Only the twins sided firmly with Mom.

Risking her family's wrath to forge her own path, Fariba decided to raise the money to attend college. As her children went off to school, Fariba went off to work. Landing a grocery store job, Fariba would stock and tidy shelves and did both with a hand and a hook.

It took her years to earn fees for college. Fariba secretly applied, and was accepted for my paralegal course. And there she was, proud and smiling from the front row.

Fariba's beauty and enthusiasm set her apart. She possessed a fiery ambition and determination seldom seen at this college. Her passion was a clear sign of someone who would not be deterred.

A few days into the course, however, I noticed that Fariba was typing with only one hand. The alarming discovery of her handicap caused me to storm the principal's office moments later.

Principal Morris also owned the college. He was an interesting human study. An observant orthodox Jew like my dad, Morris was a fine-looking bald man in his mid-forties. He had piercing blue eyes that signalled, "Don't muck with me."

But I knew his type and treated him like a brother. I also knew that in his past life, Morris was a lawyer. We had a lot in common.

"Morris, there's a young lady in my class with only one hand."

"Yes," he said casually, "I just heard about it."

Shortly after Morris hired me, he learned that I never hesitated to air my grievances and would call him out on issues of ethics and frugality. Morris' heart was all about top dollar and bottom line.

"I'm sorry, Morris. Fariba must be placed in a course where she can succeed. A course where she will have an employment opportunity when she graduates."

No answer.

I continued to press as Morris looked down at his keyboard. But the little bugger was ignoring my escalating protests, distracted by his new voice recognition software.

"She will never achieve the typing speed, Morris. Nor will she get a job as a Paralegal. Ever. And you know it," I persisted.

Again, no answer.

"This isn't a speed bump, Morris, it's a serious impediment. I know this field and so do you.

There's no room for error and no room for leniency."

I continued imploring Morris to find compassion and assign Fariba to a course in which she was more likely to succeed. He was unaffected by my plea.

"She will need to prepare legal briefs, Morris. No one will ever hire her."

"That's fine," he said, "She'll do just fine."

"But what about typing? I can't pass her."

"No, you can't. Legally, you can't pass her without the required typing speed," he said with an irritated look and a dismissive wave of his hand.

I thought: Stand up for what's right. "Morris, refund her money or put her in another course. This is unfair and unethical."

Unconscionably, Morris shook his head.

"She signed a contract. You'll teach her."

I was furious. But not wanting to further rattle Morris, I pivoted and left his office. Morris the lawyer was my employer, and I was a single mom with a rewarding career that put food on a table that could easily have been bare.

Fariba continued to study like her survival depended on it. She was earning impressive marks, but, of course, her typing speed fell short. In order to graduate, each student required a minimum speed of 60 words per minute.

With a single hand, determination and motivated by a family who repeatedly squashed her dreams, Fariba would not accept defeat. I am still astonished that she achieved 40 words per minute, a stunning accomplishment given her disability. Fariba would often stay behind to practice typing and enjoy a supportive chat. It occurred to me that she might be purposely delaying going home. Whatever her reasons, we enjoyed a wonderful information exchange, learning about each other's culture.

I came to care for Fariba in a maternal way which would have been strictly forbidden by Morris. One evening Fariba shared her family situation with me. There was discord, she said, because work outside the home contravened traditional family values.

"May I have a serious talk with you, Miss Phyllis?" Fariba asked sombrely, in contrast to her normal enthusiasm.

With graduation approaching, I knew instinctively that Fariba wanted to discuss her coveted diploma.

"We both know that graduation is soon," she said. "I can't pass without my typing speed for 60. I can only get forty, forty-one. How can I pass,

Phyllis?" She pleaded with compelling sad eyes and a voice choking back tears.

"Fariba, I can't falsify the typing score. You know that." Heartbroken, I explained that I was legally contracted to abide by the guidelines. Both my career and ethics were on the line.

"But I can't get diploma, Phyllis. And I am passing every subject, even high marks I get. I have worked so hard on this course. You know how hard I do," she insisted.

I nodded and looked at her with equal parts of compassion and pain.

"What is fair in Canada? I escaped persecution in my country to come here and everything works against me. Here, Iran, it doesn't matter. I can't become anything."

"Fariba, you're breaking my heart. You know how I feel about you and how much I care about your future. But what can I possibly do?"

"You can pass me," she said, begging, shaking and losing composure. "You know this isn't fair. You fight for people, you stand for fair. I saw you get one girl expel for cheating on test. I don't cheat. I work very hard. I get honoured marks. But I have one hand so how I get typing speed? Mine should be half required speed. That would be fair," she cried out in pain.

"Fariba, I know this is unfair. I just don't know how to fix it."

There, I admitted it. And so, the conversation ended with both of us in tears and heartbroken.

The next day, Fariba and her positive outlook returned. She asked if she could buy me a coffee after class. I reluctantly agreed. As we sat across from one another quietly sipping coffee, Fariba began.

"Miss Phyllis, I understand. You must not break rules and falsify typing score. But now I ask you to understand me a little better. Maybe how I think."

"Yes, of course, Fariba."

"You know I came from Iran with my family. We came here for a better life, to escape persecution. But life is not easy for us. We live in a small place, the whole family. We have a little food each day, nothing more.

I worked for years to make money to take this course. And they put me in your class. They see I have one hand. Why nobody tell me don't take this course?"

She knew she was breaking my heart. What she didn't know was my conversation with Morris. That I wholeheartedly agreed with her and had already fought—and lost— this battle.

"My family are now mad at me. Everyone," she continued. "They call me selfish. Stupid. They say I should not spend family money, even if I earned it. They say I will never succeed."

And then she came in for the kill. "Miss Phyllis, you know that no one will hire me. I have one hand. Look at me," she pleaded holding up her hook and reading the sadness on my face.

"They won't even interview me. You know that. I just need to graduate this course. I need to show my children, my family, that I can get diploma. That maybe, just maybe, I can be something here.

"I need to show the family that we have hope in Canada. For the twins. For my kids, Phyllis."

She just said those three little words, for my kids.

I sat sobbing before her.

"I'm begging you to pass me, just give me the minimum typing speed so I get a diploma with the rest of the guys." And then she rested her case.

My heart and my head were at war.

Dear God, whatever shall I do?

And what is ethical?

Do I honour my employment contract, which means failing and shaming Fariba? Or do I cheat the system and falsify the typing score?

I cheated the system and falsified the typing score.

Preparing Fariba's graduation diploma was an outrageously prideful moment. Fariba clocked in (falsely) at sixty words per minute and received a shiny new blue diploma along with the other students. She graduated the paralegal course with honours and Morris sucked it up.

I like to think that Morris always knew exactly what I would do. And, in the name of fairness, I felt no ethical or moral shame.

Six months later, I was at my desk marking papers when Fariba came crashing through the door.

"Miss Phyllis! Miss Phyllis!" she screamed. "I got it. I did it. You did it, Miss Phyllis." She was extraordinarily excited and I was thrilled to see her.

"I got the job! I have a job! They hire me!"

She was glowing and bouncing all over my classroom. "I got a job in a law firm. I'm a paralegal. I start work for criminal lawyer on Monday. I will be going from court to court just speaking to Judge and get remand or something. They train me.

"That's it, very small typing require!"

Running to embrace Fariba, I realized my lifetime teaching reward. I will never forget her. Not just that beautiful face but her dedication, devotion and determination to succeed. It created a shift in me.

There it was: no guarantee. Happiness, unique and personal, is only achieved by knowing what we want and having the guts to blaze past barriers.

Some encounter roadblocks and give up, while others tear them down and keep going. I'm not suggesting we break rules nor do I suggest supporting aggressive behaviour. But I am deeply inspired by a girl with one hand who never gave up.

Fariba taught me perseverance, a tool I would use with prisoners.

And my heart is still brimming with pride as I share Fariba's story. Actually, it's a story of two women whose lives and hearts touched briefly. I am honoured to have falsified a typing score in order to perform a mitzvah. In Judaism, a mitzvah is the act of doing a kindness.

A missing hand, a silver hook; the hook that captured my heart.

CHAPTER THIRTY-EIGHT

A prison divided

WOULDN'T IT BE MARVELOUS if Mr. Clean had a strong enough solution to wipe our problems away? Although we all face troubles, there is no doubt that some issues are more badass than others. I've learned through my counselling that problems vary for each of us and so does our ability to solve them in a productive, constructive way.

Here's what I know for sure. The first step to solving a problem is admitting that one exists. And a pile of Oreo cookies doesn't help solve a problem, though it can often make it worse! Take it from a professional nosher (one who snacks without cause).

The ability to determine the best solution is life changing and can also be used to help others. In this chapter, we'll go through, step by step, a mathematical problem-solving hack. You may want to bookmark this page.

Problem solving is about using imagination and logic. The best problem solvers dynamically anticipate trouble and then work to prevent it, or soften the blow. It shouldn't surprise anyone that great problem solvers possess these characteristics: analytical skills, lateral thinking, composure, the ability to influence others, creative thinking, adaptability, initiative and flexibility.

"No problem can be solved until it is reduced to some simple form. The changing of a vague difficulty into a specific, concrete form is a very essential element in thinking." – J.P. Morgan

This problem solving cheat sheet can be used personally, in complex interventions or in business scenarios.

Sequential Problem Hack

1. What's the Problem?

It may be confusing to sort out the problem symptoms from the actual problem, but it's critical to generating the best solution. If we don't understand the root problem, we may go down the wrong path.

Taking action before adequately identifying the problem is worse than doing nothing at all. So, consider the problem and, in identifying the problem, consider the following:

Who does the problem affect?
What is the issue?
What is the impact of the issue?
What will happen when the problem is fixed?
What will happen if the problem is not fixed?
When does the issue occur?
When does it need to be fixed?
Where is the issue occurring?
Why is it important that we fix the problem?
Why does it have an impact and on whom?

2. Stating the Problem

In the women's prison, one of my workshops included a group confined to segregation. Segregation at Vanier means that inmates are stuck in their cells with only two daily outings: about an hour for outdoor yard exercise and a second hour "on the range." Range time includes socialization (with strict guard supervision) and access to TV.

I was about to deliver my lesson on Critical Problem Solving when the ladies asked me to help them solve a problem that was intensifying on the range. Feeling fearless, I inhaled deeply and requested full disclosure.

There were twelve women on the unit when a problem arose with television viewing.

Group One was the News Junkies

This was a group of six ladies who wanted to watch the news. Group One claimed that updating themselves on world and local events was fundamental to their existence and acted like a crucial lifeline. It was also a ritual, they argued. Watching the daily news was a prisoner tradition.

Group two was the Objectors

The other six ladies who did not want to see the news. Because some of the women were high profile, prolific offenders, their stories would occasionally air on the news with updates. This unwelcome notoriety caused them enormous embarrassment, humiliation and shame. They claimed these news stories triggered anxiety that resulted in depression and feelings of hopelessness. They were adamant it was time for a change.

The ladies were patiently awaiting my arrival that evening to help solve their problem. First, we created a simple but concise problem statement:

"The women of Vanier have an issue with regard to their shared TV opportunity during range time. Half of the ladies want the daily news to air while the other half do not. This situation occurs every day at 5 p.m. and is causing a rise in unrest. In order to restore harmony to the segregated community, we need to determine a fair solution for watching TV on the range."

When using this problem solving model, be sure to revisit the problem statement throughout the entire process to ensure that your focus remains resolute, that the statement remains accurate, and as motivation to find a solution. Feel free to tweak the problem statement at any time.

3. Fact Finding (Research)

Once the problem is properly defined, we move into the research phase which involves collecting and recording facts, feelings, opinions and thoughts.

Before researching a solution, we must first consider the problem:

What do we already know?
What do we need to find out?

This phase may include reading books and articles, researching the internet and speaking with professionals and others who have experience in the area. In other words, do whatever and go wherever you must to gather the required information. We call this "due diligence" and it takes time.

At the women's prison, the only research available to us was a single question and answer conversation. I asked the questions, and the answers were clearly expressed by inmate Anne, a former high school teacher who was incarcerated for statutory rape.

Anne claimed that the accusing student was an extremely troubled fifteen-year-old boy who accused her in retaliation for failed grades. After extensive conversations with Anne, I chose to believe her.

Anne's backstory:

Anne proudly shared that she was a happily married with a husband, two toddlers and a pretty new puppy, all of whom were anxiously awaiting her homecoming. Her case was being appealed.

While she was in prison, Anne's parents were looking after the children at the family cottage while her husband continued his work as a human resources professional. Anne had no prior convictions and no school board violations.

At times, I would chat with Anne's mom in the reception area when she came to visit her at Vanier. The situation was heartbreaking until Anne's mom paid for a lawyer and got her daughter's life back. After a lengthy court appeal, all charges were dismissed and Anne was released from prison a year later. She is now working toward restoring her position on the school board. I love these outcomes.

In segregation, Anne was every woman's friend and my consultant. Throughout the unrest over the TV issue, Anne had encouraged the women to remain calm and approach me for a solution. She was the most reliable inmate when it came to our fact finding mission.

Below are the actual questions and answers I recorded during my fact finding phase. While Anne provided most of the answers, a few of the more disgruntled folk couldn't help chiming in.

Q - Who has control of the TV?

A - The guard who is on duty.

Q - Are the guards willing to change the channel from time to time?

A - Yes, but in a limited and rather nasty manner.

Q - Can ladies return to their cells if they experience discomfort?

A - Yes, but the guards are not warm to this 'privilege', especially if it happens often.

Q - Do ladies want alternate programming?

A - Mixed. Half want news while the other half want alternate programming.

Q - Can the TV be turned off completely?

A - Yes.

Q - What else can the ladies do during range time?

A - We are allowed to watch TV, speak quietly or request a personal phone call.

Q - Can TV time be organized with 50% news and 50% other programming?

A - Yes. I feel that the guards would agree to this arrangement.

Q - Could the news air on alternate days only?

A - Yes. I feel that the guards would agree to this arrangement.

Q - Could an inmate be assigned to control the TV?

A - No.

Q - Could a second TV be purchased?

A - No.

Q - How had the TV been previously organized?

A - In the past, the TV was always set to a local news station.

Q - Could the ladies just suck it up and face the truth if their story aired?

A – Not really, those who are seriously triggered by their story airing feel that doing so sets them back emotionally and makes prison existence unbearable.

Q - Could the ladies who are easily triggered just stay in their cells?

A - Yes. But this is seen as an unfair and inhumane solution.

Q - Do the women have access to a newspaper and is that not a reveal source anyway?

A - Most prisoners are not restricted from reading a shared copy of the newspaper. Prisoners also have access to news through visitors who relay news stories, especially those of their "cellies".

Q - If prisoners have access to a newspaper and, therefore, the same degree of shame and humiliation, then why shelter from TV news?

A - It's the audio visual TV footage that is said to cause extreme difficulty and discomfort; it's seen as public shaming.

Q - Could news continue as usual with a prisoner removing herself if and when her story is announced?"

A - Yes, this would be possible.

Prior to the brainstorming phase, all parties must agree to accept the ultimate solution. So, after much ado about viewing, the ladies agreed that once we determined the best solution, they would all comply with the outcome. A significant accomplishment for any prison gang.

4. Brainstorming

Prior to brainstorming possible solutions, we had a remedial "do not judge anyone's idea" talk. This is critical. The goal is to obtain as many creative ideas as possible, following which we would massage, evaluate and perhaps even combine them to arrive at the best solution. If an individual feels intimated or embarrassed, it could stifle a genius idea.

Outside of prison, brainstorming may be completed solo, with a fair minded friend or as a team.

Do not evaluate, judge or even consider the viability of any particular idea. Just think creatively and imagine all the possibilities without considering workability. And then, list all the proposed solutions, as seen on my blackboard.

5. Evaluating the Ideas

Now that we've recorded all possible solutions, it's time to evaluate each of them using specific criteria. When evaluating the strengths and weaknesses of each solution, consider:

Is funding a factor?
Is urgency a factor?
Does it affect our happiness?
Is there a targeted or temporary time frame?

Now evaluate the best solution. To evaluate the viability of each solution, use the rating scale below and assign a rating number.

1 – Not so great
2 – Meets some criteria
3 – Meets most criteria
4 – Best outcome for me
5 – A win for everyone

In our prison scenario, it was determined that the best solution was number 7 (an inmate would return to her cell if her story was about to air). This solution received a 5, the highest rating.

By the way, I recommend keeping your notes.

6.   Taking Action

Having agreed upon the best solution, formulate an action plan to implement it.

In solving problems, it's important to be realistic and flexible. Although most problems are solvable, few solutions are guaranteed. Even the best solution involves a measure of compromise.

But wait, in addition to good problem-solving skills, research shows that those who are always prepared to revisit and revise their original plan when necessary are most likely to succeed. Even those who believe that everything is predestined, look before crossing the street.

CHAPTER THIRTY-NINE

Integrity: Of Brilliance

MY CHILDHOOD WAS SEVERE and sadly disadvantaged. Inflicting radical religious beliefs, my father left me with hidden scars. I'm talking about the mind-crafted stuff that gets into your veins and flows through your life.

Notwithstanding, my opportunity to work in the prison system has allowed me to sprinkle goodness. This is not an accident. I believe that my childhood anguish gave rise to a profound desire to stamp out pain. For the last decade, I have amplified my voice to serve those without one. Voices often muted in shame.

Before working in the prison system I struggled to find tolerance, understanding and compassion. But after trading my legal digs for prison, the aching hearts and blind courage I found there stretched my mind to seek answers. Over time, prisoners gave me the answers that would heal me.

Rabbi David Grundland taught me that the true meaning of wisdom is the ability to learn from others. And inmates have taught me that the weakest arrow in the quiver is often the most loving. These folks know pain, are grateful for respect and embrace kindness.

My role is to provide hope and a blueprint that leads to wellness. Without hope there is no healing and no accidental success. Asking for help, my friends, is a strength and a pathway home.

A rainbow of prisoners led me to enormous growth. I am extraordinarily rich. I have learned to live as if everything is a miracle. I understand that other people hurt too. I gather patience and empathy for those who walk alongside me. And I go with a generous and forgiving heart, sensitive to hurt. My head and heart together act as a strong moral compass. And together, they take no step before negotiating what's best for me.

Life is also about balance. And so, running parallel to my work is an existential quest for pleasure; the kind of pleasure that can often be found in wildly mystic corners. Never give up on life because your story doesn't end here—and neither does mine.

This chapter is dedicated to all of us who want to reclaim joy, embrace a life of action and inaction (discipline) and reach rewarding milestones. For those who want to align themselves with their highest truth. And for those who care about humanity.

Do you think kindness is a rite of passage?

I believe how we treat people is how we will be treated; that kindness and respect are the only agencies we have over best outcomes. If you argue that kindness has no return on investment, try harder. This kindness thing is not a one and done. It's a constant awareness, an inner voice that calls upon our best. It encourages us to live our lives, not for others, but with others in mind.

Integrity is aligning our conduct with excellence. While it's nice to believe in it, when we actually treat others to human decency it's life-altering. It's an ambition powered by sheer will and does not encourage time off.

You may argue that kindness has failed. Fair enough. Some little buggers don't value kindness and prefer to perpetuate hate. But in the space between godliness and evil, we will find those who value kindness.

Ah, the art of removing toxins.

Integrity not only speaks to honesty and kindness, but to the enormous struggle it takes to achieve it even after our inevitable missteps and failed attempts along the way. Clearly, perfection is a figment of the imagination.

Even the most sainted among us have hidden secrets and colourful thoughts. We are an intentional and unintentional work in progress.

Integrity inspires authenticity, the foe of fakery. With fakery comes an agenda of manipulation. For us, authenticity is the agenda. You think honesty is tough? Silence is tougher. These days, lifelong friendships have kissed off in discord and families are hiding from one another in fear of harmony burning in Hell. My friends, we have emotional diarrhea, (outbursts of thoughtlessness). For God sakes, where are respect and diplomacy?

Expressing ourselves with love and respect while maintaining our highest level of integrity is fundamental decency. But being honest is not about being brutally honest. There is no licence for speaking without concern for feelings. Deliver your message with respect.

Integrity, serenity and empowerment mix well. So stand in your truth but do it on a foundation constructed of kindness. When we realize that our best results are tethered to the feelings of others, we strive for a universal win.

The mind is a powerful tool. Yet we spend little time improving the way we think. Let's take a moment to think about thinking. There's a connection between our thoughts, feelings and behaviour. Discipline is a wisdom that builds character.

How we think is choice, not chance. Focus on your innate ability to be fair, trustworthy and kind. When seeking a higher ground, replacing bad behaviour with good is a step closer to integrity.

Although my father was abusive and his parenting really sucked, he imparted a sliver of virtue. Dad taught us, "Never lie and always keep your word." Every time we break a promise we chip away at the bedrock of a trusted relationship. And while we may maintain the friendship, the friend loses trust. A round of applause for Dad.

Being impeccable with our word spells reliability. Do we make promises we intend to break? Don't be silly. We intend to keep our word but life shows up. So here's a plan: reduce the promises and increase the performances.

The road to integrity is paved with sincere intention. When we promise something, that promise must make the cut. This means recording every promise but never overwhelming our calendars. Make life possible and then make life work.

That phrase, "It's all about you" does not apply to us folk. Peel away the jewels and clothing because it's our ability to highlight the generosity and attributes of others that is the sweetest ingredient in a recipe for grace.

I will never forget the people who supported my passion for prison. Or those who did not.

I tell my audiences, "Don't just think nice stuff. Speak it!"

So now the inmates say:

"Drive carefully."

"Can't wait till your next session."

"Great presentation today."

I love how love is contagious.

Not everyone is wired for authenticity—don't worry about it. We'll gravitate towards those who are sensibly transparent, void of fakery and love others. Authenticity promotes bonding and encourages loyalty.

Confidence, passion and trust. These are qualities which are often seen in our most inspiring leaders. An authentic and passionate speaker looks inward before speaking outward. But passion without boundaries is folly. Because hate can be passionate too.

"Vulnerability is not winning or losing; it's having the courage to show up and be seen when we have no control over the outcome. Vulnerability is not a weakness; it's our greatest measure of courage," writes Brené Brown.

I can't think of vulnerability without crediting my thought hero, Brené Brown. In her book *Daring Greatly*, Brown describes vulnerability as "uncertainty, risk, and emotional exposure." It's that queasy feeling we get when we colour outside the lines or relinquish control with no idea of outcome. Vulnerability is raw courage. It's important to note that we are often both afraid and brave in the same moment—the very essence of courage.

The fear and bravery required to write this book are not competing. They are working as an ever present protective and motivating team.

Months ago, I joined a Facebook group for ladies who cook. I don't cook. But I thought it would be fun to break away from my writing addiction and brush with normal. I decided to take a leap of faith by asking Francine Hailman (a woman whom I had never met) to join me for coffee and cake—on her patio. That's vulnerable, right? The point is, I was both brave and afraid at the same time. Francine, your cake and company are great!

Vulnerability is not oversharing, a very different cry. Sharing an experience to help someone else gain insight is authentic. Sharing a hardship to gain pity is oversharing. Authentic people build relationships. Desperate people seek immediate relief with a premature tell-all, having complete disregard for the time it requires to build a relationship with meaningful trust. Strong people tolerate anxiety and consider appropriate sharing: to whom, how much and when.

"Vulnerability is the birthplace of love, belonging, joy, courage, empathy and creativity," says Brown. Share only with those who have earned the right to hear your story by demonstrating trustworthiness and evidence of support.

I have never understood why people lead a conversation with, "Let me be honest." Does this mean they are otherwise dishonest? Word choice is interesting and it matters. Honesty is not optional. Keeping it honest is an accepted element of integrity and moral character. Our best intentions and behaviours must couple with one another.

The strength of any relationship assumes honesty. In the absence of honesty, there will be doubt, fear of betrayal and constant surveillance. We are hard-wired to demand emotional security in our relationships. Honesty is essential in developing intimacy where bonding is the ultimate goal.

Listening is connective tissue.

Have you noticed how those who don't listen insist on being heard? Interrupting conversations is a universal itch that should seldom be scratched. People who cannot listen steer the conversation in their direction. Chronic interrupters have no idea what they're doing. For them, conversation means "game on." They leave us frustrated and feeling we may never complete a thought. Constant interrupters lack respect, display egotism and lean toward narcissism. I've been guilty from time to time myself.

Phyllis, curb your enthusiasm.

Listening and speaking should be in balance. If we find ourselves in the midst of a fast talking group frenzy, it may be necessary to bend the rules of interruption.

As a coach, I must listen to become aware of both facts and feelings. Exhibiting good listening skills gives me—or any of us— the right to be heard. I validate how someone is feeling and support them by providing options. Good listening skills are universally admired and meant to strengthen relationships. Personal, professional or romantic.

And then there's empathy. Empathy requires a deeper understanding of what someone is going through. We call it reflective listening. Sharing your problem with me is an honour and a gift. A gift that will motivate me to listen with heart and leave a beat before I speak. Empathy is the foundation of intimacy and the antithesis of selfish or self-absorbed behaviour.

Without empathy, a relationship will share time, not feelings.

People float the words empathy and sympathy as if they mean the same thing, but they don't. Feeling sympathy means we identify with a situation. We can feel sympathy for people we've never met. But sympathy is not a bonding agent and rarely a call to action—unless, perhaps, you're watching a telethon.

Empathy, sympathy's sweeter cousin, is having the capacity to identify with what a person is feeling and the ability to feel it too. Sympathy is feeling for someone while empathy is feeling with them.

Emotional intelligence (EQ) is the awareness and management of one's emotions. The more closely we connect to them, the greater our ability to feel those of others. Through learning and experience, most of us will heighten our empathy level. Not always, of course. Personality disorders such as psychopathy or sociopathy are characterized by a lack of empathy and remorse. But that's not you.

"I claim to be a simple individual liable to err like any other fellow mortal. I own, however, that I have humility enough to confess my errors and to retrace my steps," said Mahatma Gandhi.

Humility, the motherlode of all virtues, is a sign of inner strength. It's understood as an abundance of gratitude, a lack of arrogance and a modest view of oneself. Unlike accomplishments, appearances and trappings, humility celebrates and honours people.

Humble people, with an abundance of authenticity, have a gift for making others feel sunny and gay. Precious and rare, these "saints" have learned to acknowledge both their strengths and their weaknesses. We can only foster this exceptional self-assuredness when we untether ourselves from the tokens and treasures of vanity.

Humble people place the highest value on integrity. The humble man accepts failure because his intrinsic value is linked to humanity, not to success.

CHAPTER FORTY

A lesson for Miss Devine

W ITH SINCERE GRATITUDE, I celebrate a prison audience who gather each week and welcome me into their home. It's a sacred space.

The pandemic which threatened the world into lockdown ironically locked me out of prison. But long before that, prison showed me the power of humility. A virtue I forever call to mind.

Inmates consistently exhibit appreciation and respect for my work. My humility teacher was not a member of the prison population. Dena Devine, nearing fifty now, has a warm smile. But occasionally a few of her control and intimidation strategies come along with it.

As Dena begins to speak, she plants her hand firmly on her left hip and tilts her head back and to the right. With a heart of gold, or perhaps only bronze, Dena was once a tough prison guard. But rumour has it that Dena turned over her prison guard badge in exchange for an upper level office and the title of Volunteer and Educational Services Organizer after blowing out her knee in a hostage taking situation. So, Dena directs me, a reliable but unusual human who is both tender and tough at all times.

Every December, I provide Dena with an annual programming schedule for my Motivational Mondays. Dena examines my schedule and posts it for prisoners to reserve seating. While some inmates are mandated to attend class, others attend voluntarily in an effort to hope and to heal. All inmates must submit a Request to Attend Form to Dena.

Upon entering the auditorium, an inmate will often approach me and apologize for forgetting to submit his paperwork. Regulations dictate that I should send these guys back to their cells. Instead, I enthusiastically wave them on and tell them to stay and enjoy.

Shouldn't a rule make sense?

While some topics lend themselves best to a public speaking format, others are best suited to a cozy workshop layout: interactive and casual. Each topic is accompanied by a booklet authored by me, and vetted by, you guessed it, the lovely Dena Devine. Her screening process is fiercely amusing because she scours every word of my writing—but has no agency over my actual voice.

Actually, no one does. The men and I enjoy some truly riveting chats.

For the more formal presentations, I have an old laptop and a clunky projector that I won in my last divorce. Weighty equipment, I might add, which I happily schlep from home. This equipment is critical, of course, for our more formal events.

One particular Monday, a raging snowstorm screwed with my hair and makeup. An aggravating day, already characterized by a frightful hairdo and a stream of creamy pink makeup. I hate pink makeup dishevelment and have never denied this vanity. The men refer to me as "firecracker." I've never quite figured out whether this adorable nickname is intended to describe my high spirited rhetoric, or my phoney red hair.

After two hours spent navigating the snowstorm, I checked through security and was in the auditorium about to setup shop. But as I unzipped my equipment carrier, I realized that my laptop was resting comfortably at home. As the impact of this calamity came into focus, my fear mechanism kicked in. First shock, then denial. With pounding heart, I became a ditz in a dizzyingly hot room.

I had navigated a brutal storm to deliver the goods and left vital tools at home. Alone in the auditorium with my equipment deficiency, I began pacing circles round the room in an effort to calm myself and search for answers. I was secretly praying that some wizardry would drop audio-visual equipment from the sky.

My thoughts were racing: I'm in Brampton . . . too far . . . can't go back. John can't deliver. I'll wing it. I can do it.. Just do my best. Oh no. I'm screwed. This is awful . . . oh shit . . . I'm done.

A few tears later, an idea arrived from the gods: swap next week's presentation with this. Instead of presenting Friendship, (equipment reliant) do Trust, a casual workshop. Batteries not required.

Brilliant. Or so I thought.

Moments later, when my assistant Andy entered the auditorium, I explained that we needed to swap out the handouts.

"Andy, could you please run upstairs and grab the handouts on Trust. Dena's office, bottom right drawer. I'll keep the guys busy while you're gone."

Within no time, Andy returned with a shitload of Trust.

Perfect.

But (a big foul 'but') as the guys were nicely settling into Trust Yourself, Trust Others, a looming threat, Dena, flew into the room. Dena was not happy and not hiding it. Totally comfortable humiliating me in front of the boys, Dena's dreadful barrage was playing out in slow motion.

"Phyllis," and then an elongated pause. "You should know that switching the topics around messes with our calendar." This calendar represented her God.

I remained silent.

"This is completely unacceptable, Phyllis."

More silence. The room was still.

"Phyllis, please see me in my office. Right. After. Class." A public shaming announcement delivered at elevated pitch.

I was mortified. Where's my get out of jail card?

I was visibly shaken, hurt and miserably embarrassed. Never mind, I finished Trust like an adult. I could see that my guys were concerned.

When the class ended, the men were momentarily immobilized. Then, the inmates lined up to shake my hand and wish me luck. They knew that visiting the queen of punishment would not be pleasant. I later learned that everyone fears the "electric chair"—the seat facing Dena when you're facing trouble.

Assistant Andy was rose-coloured. On his way out of the auditorium, Andy cautioned me that Dena was seriously angry by using the universal "slit throat" sign.

As I headed to her office, my mind was racing, aware that Dena's "control everything" mentality was unleashed. After all, her world had been destroyed. When I arrived, Dena glared at me furiously as she ended a telephone call. Dena does not camouflage ugly or conceal nasty.

"Go stand in the corner," she demanded, stretching her arm and peering down the hallway. "I need to calm myself down before I speak with you," she announced.

Damn, she's had two hours already, this is insane. And I still have to get home in a stinking snowstorm, I thought.

My passion for prison is strong, but so was my impulse to tell Dena to just eff off. How dare she tell a grown woman to stand in a corner? I was incensed. A normal person would simply have left the building. But I headed for the corner.

Mindfulness and preparedness were out of commission. My anger was intensifying. I had a sick, nauseous feeling as my control was slipping away. But before hysteria completely overpowered me, my fairy godmother kicked up a calming veil of schmutz (dust).

Minutes later, Dena's large head emerged from her office and she motioned me in. Closing the door, Dena sat down and left me standing and foolish. Intentional?

With a face full of fury and an ugly intimidating tone, Dena said, "Do you understand that we have a serious problem here?"

I'm thinking: "Only if you say so, Dena."

"I have a schedule to follow," she continues. "The inmates only sign up for specific sessions."

I'm thinking: "Wrong, they attend every session."

"What were you thinking to switch sessions?"

I'm thinking: "Damn you, Dena, worse things happen in prison." And then, "Screw you, I'm a volunteer. The guys love me, have at it."

"What are we going to do about this, Phyllis?"

I'm thinking: "You're acting like I slept with the Warden. Which would have been far easier than preparing this damn presentation and plowing through the snowstorm from hell."

She spoke to me like I'd committed a crime against humanity. This reaction was insane.

You know I don't fold easily. I have a touch of audacity left over from my days spent crawling out of my basement window to dance in a discotheque cage. But, with my humility fully engaged, and the calming schmutz of my fairy godmother, I spoke evenly.

"Dena, please stand up."

She looked bewildered, but stood. And then she tried to stare me down. Can you imagine all this fuss over a simple schedule switch?

"It's not working, Dena," I thought. "Watch me take over."

Oh, for the gift of courage.

I began slowly, "Dena, this is not a problem. You just survived breast cancer for God sakes. You have conquered far greater challenges than a program mess. Your health is all that matters to me now. This is something we can easily fix."

She looked at me as if she had a spiritual awakening. And I exhaled an audible breath that signalled we had a truce.

"Now, please Dena, give me a hug, and let's make plans for next week."

Understand that Dena is not a pliable sidekick. It was apparent that she had been bracing for a fight. But she knew damn well that she had overreacted, and I knew damn well that cancer justifies intense compassion.

It's that integrity thing.

I saw Dena's facial muscles soften as she began to calm. She removed her hands from her hips, thrust out her arms, marshalled a smile and tilted her head to the left. Dena hugged me so tightly that my bones began to crack. It felt great.

A bond that existed professionally had just become more. Rather than defend myself, I treated Dena to some respect, perspective and kindness. When Dena began speaking, she was calm. Perhaps even grateful.

Okay. I see you cringing and questioning how humility triumphed. The answer is experience. I learned something valuable when doing research for my Difficult People session. And I learned something even more helpful in my anger management work with Tony.

As you know, thoughts inform feelings and our feelings inform our behaviour. It's an entire behavioural symphony, but here's the hack. When navigating troubled waters, find a modicum of compassion for your opponent.

And then, before you react, pause. Ask yourself: what's my ultimate goal?

In this case, my ultimate goal had nothing to do with Dena. My ultimate goal was to serve those less privileged. The men who need me. Often, our end goal has nothing to do with the person who offended us, or that moment when we felt humiliated. This approach is not easy, but it is simple—and all about fulfilling our dreams.

As I stood in the corner of that smelly hallway awaiting a spanking, I had an epiphany. Had I defended myself that afternoon, my dance with Dena could hurt hundreds and hundreds of men.

Of course I was compelled to fight back, but my higher calling is to serve the prisoners and generate hope.

As difficult as kindness is when someone offends us, the outcome counts for more. Your milestones and your goals count. Sincere compassion, kindness, and humility are enchanting. Often the right chant will land a plane and avoid the crash.

Always stay humble and kind.

EPILOGUE

Sammy's GED

I BELIEVE THE UNIVERSE has a plan. If we partner with it, a strong sense of accountability and control over outcome soon become apparent.

It is said that bad things happen to good people, but we are not victims unless we see ourselves that way. Our job therefore is to mitigate the bad and heighten the good. For ultimate fulfilment, not only must we have a desire to survive but a passion that compels us to thrive.

Ah, but how to do life when some ingredients are weak and some might actually be missing? That's exactly what this journey is about. We must discover the precious bits within and nurture the broken parts.

We make a promise to ourselves. Map the journey that puts growth on a continuum. Recognize that weakness lives in all mankind. And that how we deal with the flaws of others, how we regard others and what we do when no one's looking is key to a peaceful mind.

This oath involves striving for excellence by nurturing our inadequacies. I have only begun to recognize that my strength is also my weakness. Accepting weakness in ourselves and others is more than a virtue, it's fundamental to life and to love.

Comfort the weakness of others by taking their failings and frailties into consideration. Incorporate this into your thoughts, your words and your actions. And then, enjoy a tender heart as you project your authenticity through words of wisdom.

The best thing you can do for yourself is help others.

Yes, the universe will serve up pain, but it will also serve up joy. Pain is everywhere, but joy is often found in simple things and thoughts that feel warm. The way we choose to look at a situation is the way we shall see it. Stretch out and allow yourself to see both the good and the potential for goodness.

The commitments we make today must drive tomorrow's behaviour. Know that you have precious gifts.

You are enough.

Remember that life is a series of choices that allow us to create our story.

You are the only one who can tap in and turn on the wonders within. Look deep inside as you transform fear into freedom and scarcity into abundance. As you find your passion, you'll find your joy. Because fulfilling one's passion is what duly fortifies the flow of happiness, that precious reservoir of strength.

And now I end where I began, with tremendous humility and appreciation for those who have validated me, inspired me to do this and do more, and who have allowed me to write this book simply because they were there. You encouraged me to find my voice and put it out there with the collection of those who care.

I will continue the work I began a decade ago with prisoners. I will forever seek a deeper understanding of mankind and sharper tools to give back the blessings bestowed upon me.

During my first year at OCI, four proud and excited inmates invited me to attend their graduation ceremony. It's a yearly event! They explained that they would be receiving their GED (General Educational Diploma). You know, the high school diploma we take for granted. But for our marginalized population it's a monumental achievement.

I arrived dressed for a graduation ceremony with no idea of what "uplifting" could mean in a prison. As each man received his certificate, they narrated a horrific and humbling story of what the diploma meant to them. One story stands out.

At eleven years of age, Sammy was diagnosed with early-onset bipolar disorder. He had episodes of extreme highs and extreme lows. The latter included suicidal ideation. Sammy was prescribed serious medication, but while he was taking it, his mom was stealing it.

Sammy would run out of pills midway through each month, and he described himself as "every teacher's nightmare." Placed in foster care, Sammy was forced to babysit the preschoolers at home. Sammy's schooling was never a priority.

Mom became a drug dealer. Sammy got a limited education and a life of crime.

Finally receiving a diploma was the proudest day of his life. Holding his certificate high, Sammy's exuberance and smile of accomplishment were soul-stirring. Everyone in the room felt it.

"I'm so happy I stuck with it," he said. "Yeah, I had a few tough days . . . almost packed it in once. But hey, it's amazing how much difference a teacher can make. Mr. Waters kept me going! Never made me feel stupid. Wow, don't be shy guys, tell everyone about your goals."

"And get the help you need to succeed!"

Mr. Waters and I exchanged looks and smiled. I cried tears of sadness for Sammy's early years. And tears of pride for him now. Many prisoners work hard to find a modicum of respect and achievement in lives that afford little of each. That day, Sammy was a shining leadership star.

Not all inmates can be rehabilitated and some have unspeakable records. But what about the guy who deserves a second chance or a first incentive?

While everyone wants off the drama train, I say, let the drama begin! For my drama is in service to the damaged souls who know only a life of pain. Their suffering and their essence electrify me—and their whispers compel me to action.

And I believe that prison is exactly where I belong.

Honourable Mentions

TRISHA GLAZER

You came into my life as a proofreader and left as a friend. It never ceases to amaze me how the universe provides. Going above and beyond the scope of both proofreader and friend, your magnificence of heart is extraordinary. You are genuine and you are generous. Especially, generous. I will always remember your kindness, your expertise, and what you have taught me about the shades of life.

MYRNA RIBACK

Myrna, writing a book about my life was a "freakish fantastic" process. I am forever indebted to you for your editorial wisdom and keen insight. It's because of your efforts and encouragement that I have a legacy to pass on to my family where one did not exist. You are an absolute gift! I hope the exclamation mark is okay.

JENNIFER GERSON

Jennifer, as we sat on a cold park bench freezing our butts off in COVID compliance, you asked if I might write a book. Sometimes inspiration comes in the form of a question at exactly the right time. Without you, there would be no book. Your encouragement is a gift.

SHERRY CLODMAN

Sherry, you have been at my side since I began this manuscript. As I gave birth to the idea, you applauded me. As I struggled through months with minimal communication, you had patience with me. When I needed a push, you allowed me to read to you. And when I questioned my voice, you encouraged it by introducing me to Rebecca Eckler, who gave me a nod and a look. You clearly define and personify friendship. My appreciation is deep and my heart is full.

FRIENDS

During those dark pandemic months when we would look for a break in the clouds, your frequent manuscript inquiries served as encouragement and reinforcement. Your support has been touching and it has been unwavering. As I wrote each page, you sat on my shoulder—a collage of smiles that personify friendship. The enthusiasm and applause you provided was outstanding. The warmth and loyalty, a gift. It will never be forgotten. And to my precious Glen Rush Girls, our unexpected reunion is a miracle surpassed only by the gift of aging.

JOHN

How do I thank thee, let me count the days. Life began that moment you messaged me on Plenty of Fish. As we wiggled into each other's lives we have truly met every challenge and developed a love that is deep and meaningful. But not always easy as two crazies unwillingly mature.

As I began to work on my manuscript, you quietly did your thing too. Often you relocated to our balcony so as not to disturb my thoughts, sneaking in only for a bagel or a bathroom.

As I held my pen you held the fort.

I love you with all my heart and deeply appreciate your warmth, your kindness, your wisdom and your outstanding role as Papa John. I know you feel my love and I hope you feel my gratitude.

MELANIE

There should be a secret place in every mother's book where she gets to say something to her daughter. Melanie, you have grown into the woman I would only dare to dream of. At two and a bit you became the victim of a single parent (that would be me). But despite our bumps and bruises, we made it. You have become a shining light not only for our family but for everyone in your path. Your wisdom and generosity are outstanding—and they are widely noticed. Remember me as someone who loved you dearly with a pride that only a mother can know.

MICHAEL

Thank you for the countless times you allowed me to cut our conversations short rather than occupy your long drive home from work. It never felt good, but it often felt necessary. And for your loving support and ongoing technical expertise, which I hesitatingly admit, makes mine look rather bashful. Remember me as someone who loved you dearly, understood you, and was prouder of you than you have ever been of yourself.

FAMILY

I am a mom, gramma, sister, sister-in-saw, partner and cousin. And to you my dear family, there are no words. Okay, maybe a few. If not for family and friends we are nothing. Our family, a family of mixed race, religion and sexual orientation is a wonderful blend of good people who are tolerant and kind and loyal and loving. I hope I express my love in my behaviour because words are never enough. You exemplify respect and kindness. What more could anyone want? I love you dearly, deeply and eternally.

About the Author

PHYLLIS TAYLOR is a writer, life coach and public speaking enthusiast. But more exquisitely, she's mom to two, gramma to two, and partner to one.

Phyllis hails from Toronto, Canada where she spends a great deal of time perched on an upper floor balcony writing and blogging. Social, gregarious and fun-loving, Phyllis is passionate about both laughing and crying with friends—or just listening to podcasts.

Phyllis's only fear is making too many friends and says that her people-addiction is a real thing. Oh, how she loves problem solving and unwrapping the beauty within.

Professionally, Phyllis' career was teaching technology at a high profile international law firm. Nowadays though, when Phyllis isn't speaking, writing or counselling, she can be found entertaining the grandkids, the ladies or her beloved partner, John.

Phyllis' ultimate professional pride is her position as a motivational speaker in the prison system where she has won awards for her dedication, innovation and inspirational work. Counselling marginalized people, while guiding them on their healing journey is what Phyllis calls making her dream a reality.

You can chat with Phyllis at imagine.this@rogers.com.